Clinical Teacher Education

Reflections From an Urban Professional Development School Network

A volume in
Readings in Educational Thought
Chara Haeussler Bohan, Perry L. Glanzer, Andrew J. Milson, and J. Wesley Null
Series Editors

Readings in Educational Thought

Chara Haeussler Bohan, Perry L. Glanzer, Andrew J. Milson, and J. Wesley Null
Series Editors

American Educational Thought – 2nd edition: Essays from 1640–1940
Edited by Andrew J. Milson, Chara Haeussler Bohan,
Perry L. Glanzer, and J. Wesley Null

Forgotten Heroes of American Education: The Great Tradition
of Teaching Teachers
Edited by J. Wesley Null and Diane Ravitch

Readings in American Educational Thought: From Puritanism
to Progressivism
Edited by Andrew J. Milson, Chara Haeussler Bohan,
Perry L. Glanzer, and J. Wesley Null

Clinical Teacher Education

Reflections From an Urban Professional Development School Network

Edited by

Chara Haeussler Bohan
Georgia State University

Joyce E. Many
Georgia State University

Editorial Assistant: Jennifer M. Ulbrich, Georgia State University

INFORMATION AGE PUBLISHING, INC.
Charlotte, NC • www.infoagepub.com

Library of Congress Cataloging-in-Publication Data

Clinical teacher education : reflections from an urban professional
development school network / edited by Chara Haeussler Bohan, Joyce E. Many.
    p. cm. – (Readings in educational thought)
  Includes bibliographical references.
  ISBN 978-1-61735-423-6 (pbk.) – ISBN 978-1-61735-424-3 (hardcover) –
ISBN 978-1-61735-425-0 (e-book)
1. Teachers–Training of–United States. 2. Teachers–Professional
relationships–United States. 3. College-school cooperation–United States.
4. Education, Urban–United States. I. Bohan, Chara Haeussler, 1966- II.
Many, Joyce.
 LB1715.C575 2011
 370.71'1–dc22

                                                                    2011010596

CONTENTS

INTRODUCTION

Joyce E. Many and Chara Haeussler Bohan
Georgia State University

INTRODUCTION

Our book focuses on how to build a *professional development school (PDS) network* for clinical teacher education with partners from multiple sites in *urban school systems* serving culturally and linguistically diverse populations. In contrast, the majority of the documented experiences in PDSs have concentrated on partnerships between teaching institutions and a small number of select schools (Abdal-Haqq, 1998; Teitel, 1996, 2003). In addition, the fact that our faculty have entered into these experiences while juggling the expectations of a *research university* is also important to note. Although education faculty recognize the importance of being involved in public school classrooms (Ball & Forzani, 2009; Farkus & Duffet, 2010), the labor intensive nature of professional development school work has resulted in research institutions being slow to fully adopt a PDS approach across the entirety of their teacher preparation programs. Tenure-track faculty have often been hesitant to commit to such models in light of the demands of institutional expectations to publish or perish (Fox & Rossi, 2001). As you will see in the chapters that follow, in our PDS network, faculty, researchers, and administrators from academia and from public schools have committed to not only collaborative clinical teacher preparation and development, but also to the importance of inquiry in PDS initiatives.

Clinical Teacher Education, pages vii–xiii
Copyright © 2011 by Information Age Publishing
vii

Clinical teacher education networks in large metropolitan areas pose unique challenges as well as tremendous opportunities (Darling-Hammond, 2006; Ferguson, 1999). The most obvious challenge is the sheer magnitude of the network. In our determination to work collaboratively with all partners in our urban area, we faced additional hurdles that may not have been evident at the conception of the partnership effort. Although we understood the origins and history of the PDS movement, a large network meant that schools had varying purposes for partnering with the university. As the university partner, we had to work with all partner schools to determine a path to meet the multiplicity of desired goals (Whitford, 2005). We also faced the challenge of improving student achievement when the literature on the achievement gap continued to occupy a prominent place in the national education dialogue. The overwhelming majority of our network schools comprised high needs students from minority backgrounds.

As our network grew, opportunities to meet these challenges arose. In an effort to strengthen relationships, boundary spanners became crucial to bridging the differences between university and PDS. Field-based courses offered another venue for augmenting the partner relationship. Working to integrate inquiry in field-based sites provided opportunities for university researchers to study in clinical settings where relationships had already been established. In addition, inquiry projects helped teachers implement desired reforms in their classroom with the support of university personnel. The analysis of student achievement in the network led to the conception of focused interventions in particular classroom settings. The urban network allowed teachers and university faculty to reflect collaboratively on teacher development and high quality teaching. Finally, the large urban clinical teacher education network provided a venue for studying how to effectively manage change in both PDS and the university partner. A short description of each chapter that reveals how our clinical teacher education network met these challenges and opportunities follows.

In Chapter 1, "Understanding the Complexities Inherent in Large Scale Implementation of the PDS Model by an Urban Research Institution," Joyce E. Many, Gwen Benson, William L. Curlette, Susan Ogletree, Mary Deming, and Chara Haeussler Bohan endeavored to set the stage for how to build a large scale approach to clinical teacher education by explaining the organizational structure of our metropolitan PDS network. One of the unique challenges addressed by large-scale implementation of a PDS approach to educator preparation is the difficulty in orchestrating effective work across multiple programs and multiple districts. At our institution, we negotiated across two colleges, eight departments, undergraduate programs in early childhood education and kinesiology, post-baccalaureate programs in music, foreign language, art, and, special education, and M.A.T. programs in middle childhood education, English, social studies, math, science, reading/ESOL, and counselor education. Our partners spanned first four, then five, and most recently six metropolitan school districts. In this chapter, the authors will address our journey toward establishing coordination and communication across the multiple programs, school sites, university and school faculty and PDS coordinators, who were all working to develop relationships in our PDS. In addition, the complexities of working through business and administrative issues related to large-scale collaborative work will be addressed.

Next, in Chapter 2, "Professional Development Schools: History, Development and Current Research," Susan Ogletree contextualizes our approach to clinical teacher education by providing an overview of the professional development school movement. Professional development schools as they are implemented today emerged out of the historical context of education in the United States and have their origin in John Dewey's (1896) laboratory schools on the University of Chicago campus. After a discussion of the historical origins of PDSs, Ogletree examines the persistent historical issues of professionalism and student achievement and connects these concerns to professional development schools and contemporary issues in U.S. education.

In Chapter 3, "The Work and Insights of Professional Development School Boundary Spanners in Clinical Teacher Education," Joyce E. Many, Teresa Fisher, Dee Taylor, and Gwen Benson describe the evolution of certain individuals, *boundary spanners*, who have proved instrumental in developing trust in our PDS network. These boundary spanners bring knowledge of both the university and school contexts to bear as they facilitate the mutual understanding of participants. They serve critical communicative roles, bridge discourses, provide cultural guides, and act as change agents (Buxton, Carlone & Carlone, 2005). In this chapter, the authors explore the stories of diverse boundary spanners whose roles evolved across the course of our collaboration. The stories focus on PDS interns who became PDS teachers, PDS teachers who became Urban Teaching Fellows in our university teacher preparation programs, university graduate research assistants who transitioned to research administrators in school systems, and a school system administrator who crossed the boundary to the university to direct the entire PDS grant initiative.

Chapter 4 is "Possibilities for Clinical Teacher Education: Four Stories of Field-Based Courses Taught at Professional Development School Sites," by Mary Ariail, Caitlin McMunn Dooley, Susan Swars, and Laura Smith. This chapter reviews field-based courses in pre-kindergarten through twelfth grade (PK–12) teacher preparation programs within our urban PDS network, demonstrating that partnerships with PDSs may be implemented in a variety of ways. The chapter begins with a brief review of research support for field-based courses and includes a description of the ways field-based courses effectively address the four components of our PDS network's mission: (1) the preparation of new teachers, (2) faculty development, (3) inquiry directed at improvement of practice, and (4) enhanced student achievement. In the next section, four professors describe the field-based courses they taught (three in an elementary school and one in a middle school) in a variety of disciplines (language arts, math, and science). Each professor designed and implemented her course differently, demonstrating that field-based courses can be taught in a variety of ways to support the mission of specific PDS sites. The conclusion includes a discussion of the elements that led to successful implementation of the on-site courses.

Within our approach to clinical teacher education, we recognize both the necessity that PDS partners be cognizant of the need for the field to develop a research base on the effectiveness of PDS partnerships and the difficulties in designing partnerships with that emphasis in mind. In Chapter 5, "Examining PDS Partnerships with Survey Items: Assessing Perception of Fidelity of Implementation Using the NCATE PDS Standards," William L. Curlette and Susan Ogletree recognize that for research on the effectiveness of PDS sites to be valuable, we must begin with an understanding of the degree to which those sites reflect the PDS concept. The authors address our efforts to ensure schools in our PDS network reflect the NCATE PDS standards. To judge the awareness and extent to which NCATE PDS standards were being implemented, a survey of teachers was conducted in both our PDS and comparison schools. The results of the survey provide a critique of PDS standards and show the areas where implementation of standards was accomplished within the first several years of PDS implementation.

In Chapter 6, "Integrating Inquiry in Clinical Teacher Education Initiatives Across a PDS Network," Donna Breault, Chara Haeussler Bohan, Teresa Fisher, and Joyce E. Many argue that successful clinical teacher education partnerships should make inquiry a critical part of their work. The Holmes Group (1986) contends that inquiry provides stakeholders in a PDS partnership a culture that values each participant's work, forges professional identities, and establishes identities through which collaboration can occur. The authors identify five necessary conditions for inquiry within PDS partnerships: (a) partnerships are collective, (b) partnerships exist within educative experiences, (c) partnerships have shared purposes, (d) partnerships are active, and (e) partnerships serve significant purposes beyond themselves. In this chapter, they demonstrate how these conditions were met by sharing stories from our efforts to facilitate the use of an inquiry lens through which to approach our work. Finally, the authors make recommendations for other institutions to make inquiry a central element of their clinical teacher education relationships.

In Chapter 7, "An Approach to Increasing Student Achievement: Teacher-Intern-Professor Groups with Anchor Action Research," William

L. Curlette and August Ogletree underscore the complexities of researching the impact of professional development schools. They note that additional resources involved in a PDS implementation distributed over a school may not be sufficient to show significant gains in student achievement during the first few years. Some of the large scale PDS interventions have not shown significant student achievement (AbdalHaqq, 1988; Book, 1996; Campoy, 2000); however, a few large scale studies have shown small to moderate effects sizes in student achievement (Reed, Kochan, Ross, & Kunkel, 2001; Stallings & Kowalski, 1990). In this chapter, the authors recommend the use of a Teacher-Intern-Professor (TIP) model with Anchor Action Research (AAR). In this approach teaching-learning modules are developed by a team consisting of classroom teacher(s), intern(s), and university professor(s). The team implements the modules and then employs a quantitative or mixed methods anchor action research approach to assess student achievement. The authors give an overview of the TIP model with the AAR and then provide an example to illustrate its use. They conclude the chapter by commenting on this approach and providing some future directions for TIP model with AAR.

Understanding the impact of PDS initiatives is also addressed in Chapter 8, "Making a Difference in Teacher Development and High Quality Teaching," by Joseph R. Feinberg, Brian Williams, Dee Taylor, Kezia McNeal, Lou Matthews and Lin Black. In this chapter, the authors underscore the emphasis being placed on effective professional development via reform initiatives, district/school improvement plans, and so on. The imperative is that professional development models and opportunities must ensure ongoing high quality learning, job-embedded practice, and professional learning communities that result in teachers and administrators being able to utilize results-driven new skills. The authors exemplify current models in use in our PDS network that focus on the following: (a) how our PDS sites design and implement effective learning opportunities for both new and veteran teachers; (b) how our urban education and preparation at the university level aligns professional learning to meet unique needs of diverse districts and public school teachers, students, and organizational cultures; (c) how we integrate effective traditional learning models with new professional development designs that prepare and advance credentials of educators and improve teacher quality; (d) how to engage all stakeholders in university-school partnership learning experiences aimed at improving PK–12 student achievement and at affecting change in university teacher preparation programs; and (e) how teacher retention can be affected in high needs schools as result of effective professional learning.

As our partnership has grown and evolved over time, we have acknowledged the challenges of institutionalizing externally funded initiatives so that initiatives become part of the culture and operation of the partners involved. In the final chapter, "Partnership Building in a Context of Change," Joseph R. Feinberg, Julie Dangel, and Chara Haeussler Bohan begin with the premise that while change is inevitable when working with any public agencies, higher education institutions and PK–12 school districts are especially susceptible. Several levels of change are to be expected in a PDS partnership, including turnovers in deans, superintendents, principals, central office personnel, chairs of departments, and faculty. Indeed, teacher attrition presents significant challenges for schools, and high rates of turnover in faculty are a major factor in school staffing problems (Buckley, Schneider, & Shang, 2005). The authors stress the importance of developing a plan for change and of continuously having conversations around roles and responsibilities so that the work can continue regardless of change in personnel. Furthermore, they stipulate that developing a culture that encourages and supports new initiatives and the use of best practices can alleviate problems caused by change.

In summary, we have learned a number of lessons from our implementation of a large scale professional development school network as our model for clinical teacher education. As we think back on our collaborations as portrayed in these stories, we have reflected on how our partnership has illustrated the essentials identified as critical to PDS work by NCATE (2001). As will be seen throughout the chapters in this book, these ten essential concepts have played an integral role in the development, implementation, and success of our model: (1) time before the beginning, (2) integration of professional and student learning through inquiry, (3) placing PK–12 students at the center of PDS work, (4) learning in the context of practice, (5) boundary spanning, (6) blending of resources, (7) principal partners and institutional partners, (8) an expanded learning community, (9) the PDS as a standards-bearing institution, and (10) leveraging change. We hope that the illustrations we provide will help other educators as they draw on these elements to create their own stories of effective partnerships for clinical teacher education.

REFERENCES

Abdal-Haqq, I (1998). *Professional development school: Critical issues in teacher education*. Thousand Oaks, CA: Corwin Press.

Ball, D. L, & Forzani, F. M. (2009). The work of teaching and the challenge for teacher education. *Journal of Teacher Education, 60,* 497–511.

Book, C. L. (1996). Professional development schools. In J. Sikula, T. Buttery, & E. Guyton (Eds.), *Handbook of research on teacher education* (2nd ed., pp. 194–210). New York: Macmillan.

Buckley, J., Schneider, M. & Shang, Y. (2005). Fix it and they might stay: School facility quality and teacher retention in Washington, D.C. *Teachers College Record, 107*(5), 1107–1123.

Buxton, C., Carlone, H. & Carlone, D. (2005). Boundary spanners as bridges of student and school discourses in an urban science and mathematics high school. *School Science and Mathematics, 105,* 302–312.

Campoy, R. W. (2000). *A professional development school partnership: Conflict and collaboration.* Westport, CT: Bergin & Garvey.

Darling-Hammond, L. (2006). Constructing 21st century teacher education. *Journal of Teacher Education, 57,* 300–331.

Dewey, J. (1896) The University School. *University Record, 5,* 417–442.

Farkus, S., & Duffett, A. (2010). *Cracks in the ivory tower: Views of professors circa 2010.* Washington, DC: Thomas B. Fordham Institute.

Ferguson, R. (1999). Conclusion: Social science research, urban problems, and community development alliances. In R.F. Ferguson and W.T. Dickens (Eds.), *Urban problems and community development* (pp. 569–610). New York: Brookings Institute.

Fox, J. E., & Rossi, J. A. (2001) Promotion and tenure in a PDS partnership: A high-stakes game. *Professional Educator, 24*(1), 1–9.

Holmes Group. (1986). *Tomorrow's teachers: A report of the Holmes Group.* East Lansing, MI: Author.

National Council for Accreditation of Teacher Education. (2001). *Standards for professional development schools.* Washington, DC: Author.

Reed, C. J., Kochan, F. K., Ross, M. E., & Kunkel, R. C. (2001). Designing evaluation systems to inform, reform, and transform professional development schools. *Journal of Curriculum and Supervision, 16,* 188–205.

Stallings, J. A., & Kowalski, T. (1990). Research on professional development schools. In W. R. Houston (Ed.), *Handbook of research on teacher education* (pp. 251–263). New York: Macmillan.

Teitel, L. (1996). Professional development schools: A literature review. Unpublished manuscript. (Available from Professional Development School Standards Project, National Council for Accreditation of Teacher Educators., Washington, DC 20036).

Teitel, L (2003) *The professional development schools handbook.* Thousand Oaks, CA: Corwin Press.

Whitford, B. (2005). Permission, persistence, and resistance: Linking high school restructuring with teacher education reform. In L.Darling-Hammond (Ed.), *Professional development schools: Schools for developing a profession* (pp. 74–97). New York: Teachers College Press.

CHAPTER 1

UNDERSTANDING THE COMPLEXITIES INHERENT IN LARGE SCALE IMPLEMENTATION OF THE PDS MODEL BY AN URBAN RESEARCH INSTITUTION

**Joyce E. Many, Gwen Benson, William Curlette,
Susan Ogletree, Mary Deming and Chara Haeussler Bohan**
Georgia State University

Since the emergence of the professional development school (PDS) concept in the 1980s (Campoy, 2000; Holmes Group, 1986; Stallings & Kowalski, 1990) and the growing emphasis on university and public school collaborative efforts toward clinical teacher preparation and school reform into the new millennium (Darling-Hammond, 2006; NCATE, 2001), descriptions of the challenges encountered in establishing school partnerships have been pervasive in the literature. The importance and the difficulty of establishing trust (Darling-Hammond 2005; Ferguson, 1999; Robinson & Darling-Hammond 2005), of building relationships (Teitel, 2003), and of

Clinical Teacher Education, pages 1–13
Copyright © 2011 by Information Age Publishing

1

developing efficient and effective forms of communication (Robinson & Darling-Hammond, 2005) have been documented.

Such issues become compounded when an urban university's overall approach to educator preparation, consisting of 59 initial and advanced programs across two colleges, commits to the adoption of a professional development school (PDS) model for clinical teacher education. The scope of such an effort necessitates the development of not just individual PDS sites for a select number of cohort programs, but rather the creation of a PDS network which encompasses multiple urban districts and school sites at the Pre-K, elementary, middle, and secondary levels, and collaboration with area two-year and four year institutions. In this chapter, we will introduce the reader to how we developed a metropolitan PDS collaborative network. Specifically, we will discuss the organizational structure, roles, and methods of communication which have evolved as we have worked to increase collaboration and participation across our many partners. This network serves as the context for the initiatives shared in this book. In the final section of the chapter we introduce the reader to the stories shared in individual chapters.

AN INTRODUCTION TO THE DEVELOPMENT OF OUR METROPOLITAN PDS NETWORK

Our PDS network includes a vast array of institutions and districts in a metropolitan area, all of which share a common goal to meet the needs of a diverse student population by partnering together. Our large-scale foray into implementation of a PDS model across the entirety of our teacher preparation programs began with support from a five-year, 6.5 million dollar grant from the U.S. Department of Education. Through our collaborative work we expected (a) to increase production and retention of new teachers (especially in underrepresented groups), (b) to increase student achievement, and (c) to stimulate professional renewal for all PDS participants.

The scope of our project can be seen in part by the number of districts involved and the diversity of the student population. Our initial grant-supported network involved four metropolitan districts with averages of 36% to 75% of students on free and reduced lunch and where minority students were the majority of the student populations. The sizes of the total student enrollment for the districts ranged from approximately 50,000 for the inner city, predominately African American district to 150,000 in the state's largest metropolitan district which served a substantial population of international students. More recently, as we have expanded beyond our initial grant, we reached out not only to additional metropolitan districts but also to international urban PDS sites in China and Mexico. Throughout our work to identify potential PDS collaborators, we remained focused on our institution's mission to work collaboratively with urban partners and to try to meet the needs of underserved populations.

University partners include faculty from our institution's College of Education and College of Arts and Sciences. The collaboration has involved faculty from twelve undergraduate or post-baccalaureate programs, seven master level initial teacher preparation programs, and one counselor preparation program. We prepare an average of 500 prospective educators a year. Other participants included counselors and administrators from junior colleges and a traditionally black college. These individuals worked closely on recruitment initiatives with their institutions serving as feeder programs into many of our initial teacher preparation programs, and they implemented a scholarship program that was funded through our grant.

When we initiated the adoption of a PDS network model, we realized that a new and different organizational structure would be necessary to achieve our goals and objectives (see Figure 1.1). As Teitel (2003) notes, professional development school work requires a governance structure that "encourage(s) ownership, continuity, communication, vitality and commitment" (p. 73). To insure long term stability, as our partnership evolved we worked to institutionalize the PDS as part of our approach to unit governance, educator preparation, induction, faculty-teaching load, and coursework. To help the reader better understand this organizational structure and the processes involved, detailed discussions of the varying participant roles and methods of communications we used are presented in the following sections.

Participant Roles

As illustrated in Figure 1.1, our PDS network required identification and organization of responsible partners from both the university and public school sites. In particular, we established PDS university-based and site-based coordinators; directors for research, for budget management, and for our overall PDS grant project; and teams of university and public school faculty/administrators to guide and provide feedback on our initiatives.

A crucial component of our PDS network was the creation of university-based and site-based PDS coordinators for each site. PDS university coordinators have been drawn from both our College of Education and our College of Arts and Science faculty and these educators spend one a day a week at the PDS site. Current research (Farkus & Duffet, 2010) emphasizes that education professors believe university faculty need to spend more time in K–12 classrooms. We believe the model of having university faculty work closely one day a week in PDSs as PDS university coordinators is an ideal approach. The PDS site coordinators, who are faculty from the school

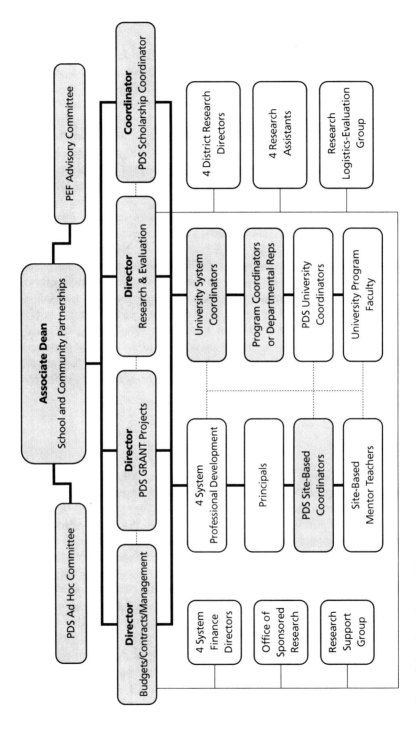

Figure 1.1 Organizational structure.

sites, typically have been assistant principals, curriculum specialists, or lead teachers from the PDS.

Together the university coordinators and their partner site coordinators have been a vital link to the success of the collaborative network. They are in touch with other school and university participants and keep lines of communication open. Drawing on both school and university expertise, they plan and coordinate a range of PDS initiatives based on site needs. As shown in Figure 1.2, these activities include pre-service and in-service professional development, induction activities, and activities designed to recruit and hire interns to work in the PDS setting. In addition, PDS site-based and university coordinators are available to interns, to university supervisors, and to classroom mentor teachers in the school. In compensation, PDS university coordinators were released from the responsibilities for up to two courses per year or were paid for a summer course load. PDS site coordinators received a stipend for undertaking the additional responsibilities.

As our PDS involvement grew, we recognized that the PDS site coordinators would be key advisors to our teacher preparation unit as we analyzed our overall effectiveness in preparing teachers for diverse settings. As a result, we reconfigured our Professional Education Faculty (PEF) Advisory Board to include all PDS site coordinators. This advisory board regularly reviews unit level data from completers of our programs and provides us feedback on the content of our program and on our assessment instruments. The inclusion of the PDS site coordinators on this board helped to institutionalize our PDS partners as integral to our overall program evaluation and accreditation process.

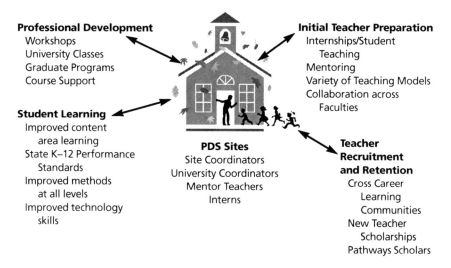

Figure 1.2 Our PDS network site based initiatives.

Students in our initial teacher preparation programs work in mentor teacher classrooms both as interns in early field experiences and as full-time student teachers. The mentors are integral to pre-service teacher development in that they provide models for teaching and help make explicit connections between teacher education and professional practice. Some PDS mentor teachers help develop teacher education curriculum and are involved in course delivery for pre-service and beginning teachers. Coordination between university and school teacher educators ensures that theoretical and research knowledge is integrated with daily classroom realities within teacher preparation programs. Depending on the program, this may happen directly at school sites as courses are field-based at the PDS site, through regular feedback submitted by mentor teachers each semester after they have hosted interns in their classroom, and/or through focus group discussions when mentors are invited to the university campus for a yearly education conference. In recognition of the important role mentors play in a PDS, mentor teachers from our PDS sites receive a stipend beyond that provided to supervising teachers in traditional placement settings.

Connections between teacher education faculty and PDS faculty are not limited, however, to interactions around initial teacher preparation programs. Consistent with NCATE PDS standards, PDS initiatives also include a focus on the professional development and support of faculty throughout their careers (NCATE, 2001). The PDS project director, system professional development directors, and PDS university-based and site-based coordinators work to identify system level and site specific needs and then to coordinate with the university system coordinators for early childhood education and middle/secondary education to involve university faculty within such initiatives. Through such a process, site-based endorsements and coursework in ESOL, math, reading, and writing have been offered to PDS teachers; in-service professional development conferences have been held at PDS sites; and ongoing professional learning communities have been established.

As an urban research institution, research and evaluation was also a strong consideration in the organization of our PDS network. Within our organizational structure, our Director of Research and Evaluation and our Director of Contracts and Grant Management work closely with the research directors of each school system. Full time research assistants are hired by the university and are employed to work in the district research office to assist in implementing PDS related evaluation. In addition, PDS teachers are paid stipends for administering yearly assessments. Finally, consultants from the public schools are hired to work on the scoring of constructed response items which are part of the yearly assessment system. Through innovative initiatives, PDS faculty and university faculty also plan and conduct inquiry projects in specific classrooms, supported by PDS mini-grant funding. The Director of Research and Evaluation and the Director of Budget and Management, along with graduate research assistants, serve as a research support group to university and public school faculty as they design and implement projects focusing on improving student achievement in PDS classrooms.

The initial grant which supported our large scale foray into PDS involvement was led by a PDS grant design team. The design team members include the principal investigator (PI) of the original grant, who was the Associate Dean of School and Community Partnerships; Co-PI's from the department of early childhood education, and middle and secondary education, who helped to coordinate activities across varying teacher preparation programs and served as University System Coordinators; the PDS Grant Project Director (a boundary spanner hired from the public school); the Research and Evaluation Director; the College of Education's Director of Grants and Contracts; and the PDS Scholarship Coordinator. Bi-weekly meetings of this team ensure implementation and coordination of grant initiatives. Over time, this group expanded to ensure representation across educator preparation in all departments in our College of Education and College of Arts and Sciences. With this expansion the design team morphed into an official committee (PDS Adhoc Committee) in the bylaws of our unit governing educator preparation, charged with envisioning possibilities and with oversight of all of our PDS work. The expanded group meets monthly to consider the long term PDS initiatives of the educator preparation programs and to evaluate the effectiveness of our PDS network. The PDS Adhoc Committee reports regularly to both the Professional Education Faculty (PEF) from the College of Arts and Sciences and the College of Education and to the PEF Advisory Committee.

Process of Communication

One of our first challenges in developing an effective network was organizing a way to deal with communication across multiple programs and multiple PDS sites across different districts. We began by scheduling regular meetings of university coordinators and PDS site coordinators. While these regular meetings helped with the communication flow, we soon realized the collaborative work integral to PDS sites would entail involvement beyond that of the site and university coordinators. For our PDS initiatives to reflect the intention of true collaboration, relationships between mentor teachers and the program faculty from specific programs had to be nurtured and developed. The challenge we faced, however, was complicated by the sheer number of potential programs which could be involved in any given PDS site. As shown in Table 1.1, from eight to ten different programs, run from one of eight departments could be involved at a single site.

TABLE 1.1 Program Specific Field Experiences

Department	Program	Elementary PDS Site	Middle School PDS Site	Secondary PDS Site
Department of Early Childhood	P–5 Elem Ed	2 days a week internships Full semester student teaching		
Department of Kinesiology and Health	PK–12 Health and Physical Education	15 day internship (undergrad) 10 day internship (grad) 10 hrs. internship adaptive PE 8 week student teaching experience	15 day internship (undergrad) 10 day internship (grad) 10 hrs. internship adaptive PE 8 week student teaching experience	15 day internship (undergrad) 10 day internship (grad) 10 hrs. internship adaptive PE 8 week student teaching experience
Department of Middle/Secondary Education	Gr. 4–8 Lang Arts/ Social Studies	Summer tutoring	Year long student teaching	
	Gr. 4–8 Math/Sci.	Fall 6 week internship	Spring student teaching	
	PK–12 ESOL	6 week internship Spring student teaching	Fall 7 week inclusion in content area 6 week internship Spring student teaching	Fall 7 week inclusion in content area 6 week internship Spring student teaching
	Gr. 6–12 English		Summer tutoring Fall 6 week	Year long student teaching Spring student teaching
	Gr. 6–12 Math		Fall 6 week	Spring student teaching
	Gr. 6–12 Science		Fall 6 week	Spring student teaching
	Gr. 6–12 Social Studies		Fall 6 week	Spring student teaching
Department of Educational Psychology and Special Education	P–5, 6–12, or PK–12 Special Education	Year long internships (typically employed on provisional certificates)	Year long internships (typically employed on provisional certificates)	Year long internships (typically employed on provisional certificates)
Department of Counseling and Psychological Services	School Counseling	Year long internship	Year long internship	Year long internship
Modern and Classical Languages	PK–12 Spanish, German, French	7½ weeks student teaching	7½ weeks student teaching	7½ weeks student teaching
Art	PK–12 Art	7½ weeks student teaching	7½ weeks student teaching	7½ weeks student teaching
Music	PK–12 Music	7½ weeks student teaching	7½ weeks student teaching	7½ weeks student teaching

In order to facilitate communication between program faculty and specific PDS sites, we developed a multi-pronged approach. First, we brought program faculty and PDS site coordinators and administrators together for a *Gallery Walk*, where faculty shared specifics related to the varying nature of field experiences embedded in different programs. University faculty prepared posters outlining their programs of study and the field experiences which occurred at different stages of candidates' preparation. PDS participants then toured the varying displays, talking in-depth with program faculty. Next, the University system coordinators from the Departments of Early Childhood Education (ECE) and Middle and Secondary Education and Instructional Technology (MSIT) and the Director for the PDS Grant Project developed a *Directory of Teacher Preparation Program Experiences*. This directory is updated and distributed on a yearly basis and outlines by school level (elementary, middle, and high school) the types of field experience placements relevant for each program. Each spring PDS site-based coordinators and administrators, PDS university coordinators, and program faculty join together in a retreat which includes opportunities for school teams to discuss with university faculty the types of intern experiences they feel would best meet the needs of their schools. After ensuring the PDS faculty and administrators have an understanding of the varying program requirements, PDS university coordinators and PDS site coordinators work together to consider school needs with relevant teacher preparation program experiences. PDS university coordinators then work closely with program faculty in departments to match the needs of programs with specific PDS sites, and they attend joint meetings with the university supervisors prior to interns' arrival at the PDS sites.

The fact that the teacher preparation programs at our institution are very content-specific, as demonstrated by the varying expectations for field experiences, did contribute to complex communication problems at school sites which housed multiple programs. This was particularly evident at the secondary level where PDSs often hosted student teachers from the varying disciplines. Different schools approached the issue in site-specific ways. At one PDS high school, the principal perceived a need for the university liaison to work across teacher preparation programs to serve as the point person for all school/university communication. At the PDS high school, the PDS university coordinator worked as a point person across subject areas. In this role as coordinator for all teacher education at the PDS high school site, the university coordinator hosted monthly meetings for all the student teacher interns, and the interns took on a school wide project of tutoring students in preparation for their end of course tests. While challenges arose, such as finding a common meeting time, ultimately the concentrated attention on marshalling the initial teacher certification interns to address needs within the high school proved beneficial for both the school and the university. Increasingly, the high school has hired the university students when they graduate and earn certification, and as these teachers gain experience, they have later been able to serve as mentor teachers to new student teachers from the university. Tighter relationships have thus formed between the university and the high school, and overall morale within the school has improved, in part because of bonds that the PDS network facilitated.

As mentioned earlier, communication from the PDS faculty also flows back from the site to program faculty from not only the PDS university coordinators but also through personal contacts when university faculty teach on campus, through formal written feedback, and through focus group discussions held on a yearly basis. This feedback leads to direct program revision. For example, difficulties were apparent in some PDS sites due to the fact that all of the subject areas within the secondary teacher preparation program had different requirements for student teaching. In other words, the science initial certification program had different requirements and expectations than the English program, and the social studies program differed from the math program. The tensions caused by the variation within the university teacher education programs served as a catalyst to help the teacher education faculty reflect and work to develop some uniformity across content area teacher certification programs. Ultimately, the university developed a common teacher education handbook, with common guidelines and expectations for middle and secondary teacher education programs.

Similarly, communication from PDS elementary faculty also led to direct changes in the supervision process in the early childhood education program. The undergraduate ECE program contains four blocks with varying field experience requirements. As a result, PDS site faculty often found themselves trying to communicate with four different ECE supervisors as well as the university coordinator. In light of PDS faculty recommendations, the program moved to a vertical supervision model where a supervisor was assigned to a specific site and was responsible for interns in that site regardless of the blocks in which they were enrolled. This model increased the ability of PDS faculty to develop relationships with particular university supervisors and enable the supervisors to have a school-wide perspective of interns' experiences.

Another set of communication processes were aimed at increasing the knowledge of PDS initiatives across the large number of university and public school faculty who might not be directly involved in PDS work in a given semester. We believed that in order for us to develop a PDS network which truly exemplified a collaborative effort, we had to move beyond involving a small group of committed individuals and instead ensure a ground-swell of interest and engagement in our model. Given the number of programs at the university, and the number of school sites involved, we had to maximize our efforts to inform faculty in both contexts about our work with the hopes of moving them from the periphery into the midst of our efforts. To achieve this end, we began with the production of a quarterly PDS newsletter. Newsletters highlighted collaborative projects between the partners, such as math family nights, field-based courses, inquiry projects, and state and national presentations. In addition, information about mini-grants, scholarships, and travel support was shared. These newsletters were distributed both in emails and at university and public school faculty meetings. As a result, program faculty expanded their knowledge of the initiatives which were being undertaken and PDS sites were inspired and motivated by ideas shared by PDS partners in neighboring systems.

In addition to the newsletters, the Director of the PDS Grant Project also produced a PDS video that showcased the exemplary programs and collaborative efforts of PDS partners. This video was shown at university meetings and candidate orientations, placed on the PDS website, and made available to PDS partners for use at school and community functions. By working to publicize our efforts at collaborative work, we have increased the knowledge and understanding of university and public school educators and provided opportunities for celebration of what we have accomplished together.

TAKING CLINICAL TEACHER EDUCATION TO THE NEXT LEVEL: NETWORK FOR ENHANCING TEACHER QUALITY

Following the end of our initial funding, we submitted and secured additional federal funding to further expand our PDS network and clinical teacher education initiatives. The new project focuses on developing a *Network to Enhance Teacher Quality (NET-Q)*. Through this grant, we have been able to include 24 professional development schools in the new network. The PDS sites from the previous grant were encouraged to apply and were given extra points on their applications. It was important to us to maintain the current network of schools that have partnered with us over the last five years but also give them an opportunity to opt out of the network if desired. At the same time, we expanded our scope to incorporate new metropolitan systems into our network and to support other state institutions to develop a PDS approach to their clinical teacher education programs, especially those serving high needs schools in their surrounding areas. The NET-Q partnership includes participation by six metropolitan school districts, 19 rural districts, three four-year institutions (including two historically black universities) and one two-year institution.

Our new NET-Q project addresses the following priorities: (a) reform of pre-baccalaureate programs, (b) establishment of teacher and leader residencies, (c) collection and use of student achievement data to assess teacher preparedness and performance, and (d) provisions for continuous improvement to teachers. Within these priorities, we have embedded initiatives proven to be effective in our prior work. These initiatives include induction activities through the development of Cross Career Learning Communities (CCLCs) for new and veteran teacher support and retention, inquiry and professional development through our Teacher Intern and Professor (TIP) model, action research/inquiry projects, and competitive research fellowship mini-grants, and a Georgia Public Broadcasting Digital Partnership Collaborative to provide professional development leading to endorsements for teachers.

Through our partnership with the National Commission on Teaching and America's Future, teaching residents, mentors, and university faculty will also be participants in a Teachers Learning in Networked Communities (TLINC) online community of support. The TLINC online communities will connect our teacher residents with other teacher residents across the country. These communities build proficiency with learning technologies and establish the habit of participating in a collaborative teaching culture that teachers will carry with them throughout their teaching careers.

In summary, implementing a large-scale PDS network is complex process. To ensure success of our network, we have worked to develop new organizational structures, roles, and communicative processes. Consistent with previous literature on creating and sustaining PDS partnerships, these developments have been crucial in ensuring the success of our approach to clinical teacher education (Teitel, 2003). The structures we put in place have supported the relationships which developed through the interactions of the individuals involved. As a result, we have been able to establish the collaboration and trust necessary for effective university-school partnerships (Wiseman & Nason, 1995; Robinson & Darling-Hammond, 1995). We recognize, however that such large scale implementation could not have been possible without financial support. In order to ensure the stability of our partnership in the difficult economic times faced by our state during the years our partnership has evolved, we have learned the importance of leveraging funds from both federal and private sources. Together our university and district partners identify the key initiatives that have been crucial in our success, and we target funding opportunities which are matched to these initiatives. In this way, we have been able to scale up our professional development school model and we hope to continue to support this network in order to provide a foundation for collaborative clinical teacher education and educational research in urban settings. Ultimately through this approach, the university faculty, public school faculty, and prospective educators are working together to make a difference for the education of students in our urban communities.

REFERENCES

Campoy, R. W. (2000). *A professional development school partnership: Conflict and collaboration.* Westport, CT: Bergin & Garvey.

Darling-Hammond, L. (2005). *Professional development schools: Schools for developing a profession.* New York: Teachers College Press.

Darling-Hammond, L. (2006). Constructing 21st century teacher education. *Journal of Teacher Education, 57,* 300–331.

Farkus, S., & Duffett, A. (2010). *Cracks in the ivory tower: Views of professors circa 2010.* Washington, DC: Thomas B. Fordham Institute.

Ferguson, R. (1999). Conclusion: Social Science research, urban problems, and community development alliances. In R. F. Ferguson & W. T. Dickens (Eds.), *Urban problems and community development* (pp. 569–610). New York: Brookings Institute.

Holmes Group. (1986). *Tomorrow's teachers: A report of the Holmes Group.* East Lansing, MI: Author.

National Council for the Accreditation of Teacher Education. (2001). *Standards for professional development schools.* Washington, DC: Author.

Robinson, S. & Darling-Hammond, L. (2005). Change for collaboration and collaboration for change: Transforming teaching through school-university partnerships. In L. Darling-Hammond (Ed.), *Professional development schools: Schools for developing a profession.* (pp. 203–221). New York: Teachers College Press.

Stallings, J. A., & Kowalski, T. (1990). Research on professional development schools. In W. R. Houston (Ed.), *Handbook of research on teacher education* (pp. 251–263). New York: Macmillan.

Teitel, L. (2003). *The professional development schools handbook.* Thousand Oaks, CA: Corwin Press.

Wiseman, D. L., & Nason, P. L. (1995). The nature of field-based teacher education experience. *Action in Teacher Education, 17*(3), 1–12.

CHAPTER 2

PROFESSIONAL DEVELOPMENT SCHOOLS

History, Development and Current Research

Susan Ogletree
Georgia State University

A professional development school (PDS) is a collaboration between a school (including its teachers, administrators, staff, students, and supporting community), that school's system or district, and a postsecondary teacher-preparation institution—a college or university providing pre-service and in-service training to individuals within the school. By working together, all partners supporting the professional development school hope to create enriching academic experiences for students, to provide supportive, professional development for teachers, and to assess the effectiveness of instructional practices.

Professional development schools as they are implemented today emerged out of the historical context of education in the United States. Contemporary professional development schools have their origin in John

Clinical Teacher Education, pages 15–32
Copyright © 2011 by Information Age Publishing
15

Dewey's (1896) laboratory schools on the University of Chicago campus. Dewey's schools provided pre-service teachers the opportunity to work in a classroom environment with master teachers, who modeled progressive instructional techniques. The schools also provided the opportunity to evaluate and document teaching methods to determine which methods work best with students (Campoy, 2000). These interests in collaborative teaching training and research for instructional improvement are characteristics of today's professional development schools, but the laboratory schools and professional development schools differ in an important way: Dewey's laboratory schools were administered by the university, but a contemporary professional development school is administered by an equitable partnership of the participating school, system, and university.

HISTORICAL ISSUES

Over the course of the twentieth century, several sociopolitical movements influenced the development of educational systems in the United States, and contemporary professional development schools address two of these specifically: the professionalization of teaching and public concerns regarding student achievement. Although we present these issues separately, they are interrelated, each affecting the other, particularly as the late-century accountability movement led educational policy and U.S. schools into the *No Child Left Behind* era of the early 2000s.

Professionalization

In 1920, the Carnegie Foundation for the Advancement of Teaching (1920) published what became known as "The Learned Report," named after chief author Charles Learned. The authors of the report recommended that teacher education become a professional, evidence-based clinical preparation program similar to that recommended by the Flexner (1914) Report for the practice of medicine (Imig & Imig, 2005; Levin, 1992). This recommendation would require strengthening teacher preparation in the United States and would end the practice of allowing untrained individuals to teach (Darling-Hammond, 2006).

One of the most important recommendations made by the Learned Report was that all teachers be required to participate in a 4-year prescribed teaching curriculum. The idea was not only to become proficient in the subject matter but also to learn pedagogy, the art and science of teaching. Future teachers were expected to attend a college whose main focus was that of preparing future educators, and faculties at those educational institutions were expected to work with prekindergarten through twelfth grade (PK–12) schools to produce teachers with full knowledge of the "scholarship of teaching." The Learned Report envisioned that professional schools of education would be held in equal esteem as those that prepare doctors or lawyers. However, during the subsequent 85 years, the Learned Report and its recommendations disappeared from teacher education reform discourse (Imig et al., 2005).

Later in the century, the Carnegie Forum on Education and Economy (1986) recommended the establishment of a national board for professional teaching standards. This recommendation represented an effort to enhance the prestige of the teaching profession through recruitment of more academically able candidates. Toward that end, the Carnegie Forum also recommended the establishment of clinical schools, which would serve to prepare teachers to meet the new standards and which would link college of arts and sciences faculties and college of education faculties to prepare PK–12 teachers. The clinical schools would provide PK–12 teachers with collaborative access to college faculty with extensive content and pedagogical knowledge.

The Carnegie Forum on Education and Economy (1986) also recommended that professional teacher training be taught at the graduate level, following the teacher candidate's completing of a bachelor's degree in an appropriate content field, as did the Holmes Group (1986). These ideas mirrored preparation for recognized professions, such as medicine and law. Initially, they were widely embraced, but by the late 1990s, social and economic realities at teacher preparation institutions led to the retention or reinstatement of undergraduate teacher preparation programs (Newman, 2006). While the National Board for Professional Teaching Standards does provide professional certification for teachers (generally after they have completed graduate-level studies in their field), entry into the field of teaching itself remains in the control of state boards of education and/or professional practices commissions instead of in the hands of educators themselves.

Student Achievement

With the publication of *A Nation at Risk* by the National Commission on Excellence in Education (1984/1992), the U.S. public was made aware of the plummeting achievement test scores of both college-bound and non-college-bound students. Based on standardized test results, both segments of the population were mastering less of the academic subject matter than students from the previous decades. The Commission described U.S. educational performance as "a rising tide of mediocrity" that threatened the educational foundation of American society. As a result of *A Nation at Risk* and other publications, state and local commissions of excellence were created to examine the educational problems. These commissions recommended changes in school curriculum, graduation requirements, teacher certification, and assessment (Stallings & Kowalski, 1990).

Business and industry leaders were also concerned about the decline in education. They declared a need for employees who were proficient in basic skills and able to transfer knowledge from one situation to another. They also wanted employees with a thorough understanding of information acquisition through the use of computers and expanded technology, and they demanded that public education produce graduates with these characteristics. Developing this type of high school graduate and restructuring the schools for the 21st century required a new paradigm, including construction of a new and different system of teacher education (Levin, 1992; Stallings et al., 1990).

The Carnegie Forum on Education and Economy (1986) and the Holmes Group (1986) encouraged the reconceptualization of teacher education at the university level. The Holmes Group (1986, 1990, 1995) recommended that universities move toward a collaborative model of professional-school partnerships linking colleges of education with PK–12 schools, where inquiry and action would come together in reflective practice (Levin, 1992). They also recommended that teachers in the field should have stronger backgrounds in their content knowledge fields.

In addition to the Holmes Group (1990), many national organizations and smaller initiatives have supported the subsequent professional development school movement. For instance, the professional development school concept has received national support from the American Association of Colleges for Teacher Education (AACTE), the National Council for Accreditation of Teacher Education (NCATE), and the National Center for Restructuring Education, Schools, and Teaching (NCREST)(Teitel, 1999). By improving teacher preparation and by researching teaching practice, professional development schools should lead to an increase in student learning as measured by academic achievement tests.

CONTEMPORARY ISSUES

Professional development schools connect to a number of contemporary issues in U.S. education, in addition to the persistent historical issues of professionalism and student achievement. These include teacher retention, encouraging new teachers to remain in teaching positions for five or more years; and teacher shortages, which have led to the widespread but problematic implementation of alternative licensure programs.

Teacher Retention

Attrition rates for new teachers are very high, with many researchers finding that between 25–50% of them leave within the first few years of entering the profession (Georgia Partnership for Teacher Education, 2006; Grissmer & Kirby, 1987; Guarino, Santibanez, & Daley, 2006). Many leave the profession because they have not felt they connected with their students, because they have experienced a sense of frustration, or because they considered themselves failures in the classroom (Johnson & Birkeland, 2003). Nationwide, teacher attrition costs over $2 billion annually (Fulton, Yoon, & Lee, 2005).

In a review of the professional development school internship literature, Abdal-Haqq (1998) concluded that novice teachers from PDS placements are better able to use varied pedagogical methods and practices in the classroom (Hallinan & Khmelkov, 2001; Zeichner, 1992). PDS-trained novice teachers are more reflective in their practice and are more knowledgeable of school routine and activities (Trachtman, 1996). PDS-trained novice teachers are more confident in their knowledge and skills as professionals and are better equipped to instruct ethnically and linguistically diverse student populations (Book, 1996). They are also more likely to take a full-time teaching job in an inner-city school when they complete their practicum in urban areas and remain in the profession (Arends & Winitzky, 1996). Professional development school teacher-interns demonstrate strong preparation, high self-confidence, and the benefits of experience, characteristics that improve the likelihood that they will remain committed to their teaching positions.

Teacher Shortages

A shortage of qualified teachers is a frequent, cyclical occurrence in U.S. public education (e.g., Fowler, 2009) in which school systems cannot find qualified individuals to serve as teachers in their schools. Although recent downturns in the economy have reduced teacher shortages, in math, science, and special education, teaching positions remain understaffed. The return to a robust economy likely will mean across the board teaching shortages, especially in urban and rural schools. The alternative certification movement was established in direct response to teacher shortages in an attempt to ease the entry into the teaching field from other professions (Stafford & Shaughnessy, 2006). The shortage of teachers, coupled with the lack of public confidence, led 41 states to provide a licensure route that excluded the student teacher experience (Frasier, 1994). Policymakers supported shortening or removing traditional student teaching by arguing that on-the-job supervision is more effective in preparing teachers to teach. This truncation of preparation saves training dollars and places student teachers into the classroom more quickly; however, Wright, McKibbon, and Walton (1987) found that pre-service teachers participating in the alternative certification process appeared to lack needed classroom skills. Additionally, Darling-Hammond (1992) found that teacher education programs with little or no student teaching experience leave recruits significantly underprepared in areas important to classroom effectiveness.

Problems with alternative certification programs can be directly linked to reform leading to growth of the PDS movement (Dixon & Ishler, 1992), as professional development schools include prolonged student teaching opportunities involving focused supervision in the classroom (Williams, 1993). Professional development schools provide an improved student teacher experience, the results of which should increase public confidence in the preparation of teachers.

DEVELOPMENT OF CONTEMPORARY PROFESSIONAL DEVELOPMENT SCHOOLS

Professional development schools were originally conceived as teaching communities housed in regular schools that would connect colleges of education with PK–12 practitioners. The school-university collaborative would seek to develop excellent learning programs, thought-provoking teacher preparation, professional development for all participants, and research projects to enhance pedagogical knowledge (Campoy, 2000), ideas similar to the ones expressed in the Carnegie Forum on Education and Economy (1986). The collaborative partnership also sought to bring together teacher candidates, practicing teachers, administrators, and university faculty for rich, engaging discourse. Goodlad's (1994) National Network for Educational Renewal, NCREST, and NCATE agreed upon four basic goals that PDSs must pursue:

1. Provide a clinical setting for pre-service education
2. Engage in professional development for practitioners
3. Promote and conduct inquiry that advances knowledge of teaching
4. Provide exemplary education for PK–12 students (Clark, 1999; Teitel, 1999)

Teitel reported that collaboration, reform, and renewal are the three most important strands used to develop the PDS movement. It was in the 1980s that collaboration among faculty members became an important part of educational reform. The next logical step in collaboration was creating partnerships across institutions, such as between school and university, to engage complementary expertise and create a working synergy that allowed both partners to expand their educational boundaries while challenging accepted educational practices that are the basis for teacher decision-making in the classroom (Pugach & Johnson, 2002). Work within the PDS movement has confirmed that there is also a synergy between collaboration and learning (Neapolitan & Scott, 2004). The inclusivity of collaborative partnerships increases energy and joint ownership in the partnership (Pugach et al., 2002). Collaborative partnership building between school and university can also be used to create an environment for resolving tensions historically existing between them (Sewell, Shapiro, Ducett, & Stanford, 1995), such as the rhetorical dichotomy between theory and practice (Stoddart, 1993). Pre-service teachers often report being frustrated to find classroom settings dissimilar to those studied in educational methods courses, but a collaborative environment, such as that in a professional development school, combines theory and practice *in situ*, allowing the student teacher to construct meanings from multiple sources and gain immediate feedback. Additionally, the school's and university's collaborative relationship promotes exploratory discussion so that mutually acceptable approaches to solving problems can be found (Wiseman & Cooner, 1996).

According to Darling-Hammond (2005), current PDS reform efforts within schools and universities require exceptionally skilled master teachers because new teachers entering the workforce must now possess the skills to motivate and educate all students to their highest level of academic performance. They must accommodate, celebrate, and respect student diversity while ensuring that all students learn to create, present, and synthesize their own ideas. To accomplish this end, teachers are required to have a clear understanding of learning as well as teaching while connecting student experiences with curriculum goals. More complex forms of teaching are required to support the wide range of learning styles and multiple intelligences encountered in the classroom. The ability to teach higher order thinking skills and to enhance student performance abilities are now expected from beginning and experienced teachers (Darling-Hammond, 2005).

An authentic professional development school moves beyond relationships between supervising teachers and student teachers and affects the overall environment of professional practice. It encourages continuous inquiry, collaboration, collective work, and professional collegiality. One important feature of a professional development school is the shared decision-making in teams within school and between schools and universities in an effort to discourage teacher isolation and to increase knowledge sharing, team planning, and collective reflection between and among all participants (Darling-Hammond, 2005).

Efforts have been made to standardize the definition and goals of a professional development school. NCATE initiated a project in 1995 to develop such standards for PDSs. Obtaining a clear definition of what comprises a professional development school was challenging because there was little agreement among schools which called themselves by the name. Some continued to prepare teachers in the traditional manner (but called student teachers "interns" so they would sound professional). Other professional development school partnerships worked to improve teacher and student learning through a major shift in the student teaching process and in the collaborative relationship between the school, university, and, when present, district or system (Levins & Churins, 1999). The final NCATE (2001) standards address several characteristics of professional development schools: (a) learning community, (b) accountability and quality assurance, (c) collaboration, (d) equity and diversity, and (e) structures, resources, and roles.

RESEARCH ON PROFESSIONAL DEVELOPMENT SCHOOLS

As the number of professional development schools in the United States has grown, so has the number of studies being conducted on them. These studies address the theory, implementation, and description of professional development schools, and many explore the nature and impact of district-school-university partnerships (Abdal-Haqq, 1998; Book, 1996; Campoy, 2000). However, Stallings and Kowalski (1990) found that while the number of professional development schools has grown, there has been little *systematic* evaluation of them. In 1996, Abdal-Haqq reported that a majority of the PDS research conducted had focused on outcomes associated with pre-service and in-service teachers. The research usually explored their satisfaction with teaching as a profession, teacher efficacy, perceived competence, and attrition. Book pointed out that most PDS research has been descriptive, with little methodological detail included. The lack of detail raises questions about the transferability or replicability of the studies. Abdal-Haqq identified a need for more research on the effect of professional development schools as they specifically relate to student academic achievement.

Because a professional development school is involved in a variety of partnership activities, such as pre-service and in-service teacher training, professional development of novice and experienced teachers, action research, and academic achievement of students, evaluation becomes complex. The difficulty in isolating PDS effects from other confounding variables makes it hard to determine if programs are clearly successes or failures (Book, 1996; Campoy, 2000). Consequently, evaluators of professional development schools tend to use qualitative methods that are primarily descriptive in nature, including interviews, questionnaires, journal writing, field notes, and classroom observations. There have been many case studies conducted in professional development schools, and these studies usually focus on particular networks, such as National Network for Education Renewal (Osguthorpe, Harris, Harris, & Black, 1995) and the Benedum Collaborative (Hoffman, Reed, & Rosenbluth, 1997), or large collections of professional development school studies (Darling-Hammond, 1994; Petrie, 1995).

Book (1996) suggested the complexity of the school and classroom environments and the multitude of possible interaction factors cause descriptive methodologies to be predominantly used in PDS research. A thick description by the researcher of the complexity of interactions in the school and classroom gives the reader a clearer understanding of the PDS educational process. The use of descriptive methodologies allows the researcher to document the nuances in the evolution of partnerships among system, school, and universities. Ultimately, the PDS goal of promoting inquiry within the school setting is more conducive to the use of qualitative methodologies. However, educators are currently pressed by the business, political, and civil sectors to provide quantitative analyses of educational programs, such as data concerning student pass rates, standardized achievement test scores, and retention rates for students. These sectors also call for measurement of the outcomes of teacher education programs, including the number of teachers certified to teach, how long they stay in the profession, standardized test performances, performances as first-year teachers, and the impacts teacher education graduates have had on the students they teach (Houston, Hollis, Clay, Ligons, & Roff, 1999).

A decade ago, Abdal-Haqq (1998) reported that there was little conclusive evidence that PDS programs improve student achievement. One possible reason for this is that inquiry and student achievement have been the two areas least systematically researched. The studies that have been conducted do not give a clear and concise description of teaching and learning activities that take place within the PDS program. Thus, the link between teacher development and student achievement has not been clearly identified and researched. According to Abdal-Haqq (1998), a continuing lack of convincing data could lead to the demise of professional development schools.

In response to the lack of achievement data, Teitel (2001a) provided a current review of PDS research focusing on outcomes for pre-service teachers, effects of professional development on experienced teachers, and the impact of the PDS model on student achievement. Teitel suggested that the body of research surrounding student achievement in professional development schools is growing. For instance, Judge, Carriendo, and Johnson (1995) reported an increase in math score gains in one urban elementary PDS in Michigan, and Wiseman and Cooner (1996) described dramatic increases in scores on the writing portion of a state achievement test through a PDS "writing buddies" program. Knight, Wiseman, and Cooner (2000) reported an increase in the percentage of students mastering a state criterion-referenced test in mathematics for third and fourth grades following implementation of a professional development school intervention.

Teitel (2001a) identified two of the most comprehensive and convincing large scale studies of the impact of professional development schools: The Benedum Collaborative Model of Teacher Education (Gill & Hove, 2000) and the Houston Consortium (Houston et al., 1995). These studies and one other, the metropolitan area professional development school partnership that is the basis of the remainder of this book, are summarized below.

The Benedum Collaborative Model

The Benedum Collaborative Model study led by J. Webb-Dempsey of West Virginia University (WVU) focused on the effects of a PDS program implemented in 12 urban school systems on student achievement. Establishment of PDSs in the local public schools was coupled with a review of WVU's teacher education program during which the entire curriculum was reinvented by moving from a 4-year bachelor's degree program to a 5-year program that including graduate-level training, by adopting more demanding admission requirements, and by assigning each novice teacher to a professional development school site for three consecutive years.

Evaluation data included interviews with 400 students, surveys of 3,000 students, data collected by the state's department of education, and standardized achievement tests. The 21 professional development schools in the program were compared with state and county averages of attendance, graduation rate and achievement test scores (Teitel, 2001b). In 1999, mean basic skills scores on the Stanford Achievement Test (9th ed.) were higher in professional development schools than in other schools for students in grade six. Additionally, scores on individual tests within the achievement test showed PDS students with the largest gains in mathematics (although differences that have a substantial magnitude may not achieve statistical significance). The researchers felt it was more appropriate at that stage of implementation to examine the magnitude of the differences than to seek statistical significance (Gill et al., 2000). Thus, the discussion of gain difference focused on effect sizes rather than significant differences. The final analysis of data showed a slight increase in attendance and graduation rates with no significant difference in achievement (Teitel, 2001b).

The Houston Consortium

The Houston Consortium researchers used a quasi-experimental model combining test score data with qualitative observational methods. Using data obtained from four universities and three school districts, the study compared test scores of PDS and non-PDS participants on the Texas test for certifying new teachers and student test scores on the Texas Assessment of Academic Skills (TAAS). Classroom observations were also used to document instructional time on task. Consortium teachers were found to have higher certification test scores, to spend more time checking student work and responding to students, and to encourage student self-management and positive behavior that led to improved student performance (Houston et al., 1999; Teitel, 2001b).

With regard to student achievement, of the 16 participating PDS elementary schools, 14 showed an increase in reading, while two showed a decrease. In mathematics, all 16 PDS sites showed an increase. As measured by the TAAS, writing skills increased in ten of the schools and decreased in eight of the schools. In these schools, pre-service teachers taught math and reading to small groups and individual students, but they did not teach writing.

The Houston Consortium researchers concluded that there were significant positive changes in student achievement over the two-year period. It appears that during the first year of a Houston Consortium school's becoming a PDS, the changes were the greatest. During the second year, achievement gains appeared to stabilize but were still higher than scores in the school before it became a PDS. The Houston Consortium conducted both formative and summative assessments on the program's impact on student teachers and PK–12 student achievement. The overall research results tended to be supportive of program effectiveness in both educating teachers and student achievement (Houston et al., 1995)

The Professional Development School Partnerships Deliver Success (PDS2) Program

In 2004, our own institution, a large research university in the southeast, received a federal grant to implement professional development schools across four high-needs urban school systems with Dr. Gwendolyn Benson as the project investigator. The project employed a quasi-experimental design to compare 12 professional development schools to 12 comparison or control schools in these school systems. The PDS² schools were matched with control schools on student achievement and student characteristics as measured by a student survey at the beginning of the grant.

The project measured student achievement in two ways: using a specifically designed construction-response instrument, and using the state Criterion-Referenced Competency Test. The PDS coordinators and the district research associates cooperated in matching two sets of data by students. While an increase in middle school mathematics scores was shown, it was difficult to obtain the project's goal of a 3% increase in a standardized test score over the course of a year. This difficulty gave rise to the Teacher-Intern-Professor (TIP) model, which was implemented during years four and five of the grant. The TIP model allowed for a closer examination of the direct effects of interns and professors on the academic achievement of students in a themed TIP classroom. Preliminary data suggest that use of the TIP model can lead to a significant difference in test scores and ultimately student achievement for a particular classroom (see Chapter 7).

While other areas, such as teacher induction and teacher efficacy, were studied, the most notable finding was in the area of teacher retention. During year two of the grant, cross career learning communities (CCLCs) were introduced as a method to increase teacher retention and improve classroom pedagogy. The CCLC model is the framework for teacher learning communities where classroom pedagogical questions and student learning issues are brought to the group for problem solving. The CCLC model includes pre-service teachers as well as teachers with multiple years of experience, and it is within this framework that professional development work is conducted. Systems that implemented the CCLC model showed a significant increase in new teacher retention rates.

Other Student Achievement Research

As the PDS movement grows and matures, research is being conducted more scientifically in an effort to show student academic achievement impact or lack thereof. The movement toward a more scientific approach supports continuous efforts to improve the quality and persuasiveness of all educational research (Cook, 2002; Riehl, 2006; Slavin, 2004). Since the enactment of the *No Child Left Behind Act* of 2001, there has been a stronger focus on student learning outcomes throughout the U.S. educational system as well as in the PDS movement. The use of high-stakes standardized tests has forced U.S. schools to demonstrate measurable student outcomes when attempting to validate innovative programs or models. This new accountability (Fuhrman, 1999) places the impetus upon student performance and the locus of responsibility for performance directly on local schools. The growing expectation that local schools meet the academic needs of a much more diverse group of students to much higher predetermined standards creates much greater demands on teachers (Darling-Hammond, 2000). The new accountability also includes the use of public reporting of student outcomes, rewards, and sanctions to encourage change in "failing" schools' curriculum and instructional practices (Fuhrman, 1999; McDonnell, 2004). While the Obama Administration has indicated a move away from some of the strictures of the *No Child Left Behind Act* of 2001, state policies and educational practice continue to stress the importance of educational assessment based on student achievement scores as a critical outcome.

Systematic research that evaluates professional development school implementations' relationship to student achievement outcomes have not produced strong results, although results typically support the PDS implementation. In 2004, Teitel updated the NCATE professional development school review of research, and the section on student outcomes identified 14 exemplary studies. These studies, some of which are described below, attempted to make connections between changes taking place in the professional development school and student achievement primarily through the use of standardized test data.

In one such study, Pine (2003) reported single-site longitudinal data for an elementary school in Pontiac, MI. When test scores were compared with other schools in the district and state test scores, the Pontiac elementary school, over an eight-year period, met or exceeded the state and district averages. Pine attributed their success to a focus on student learning by the professional development school.

In a two-year study of an urban San Diego professional development school, Frey (2002) reported an overall increase in reading scores of 31% on the SAT-9 tests with 55% of seventh graders scoring above grade level. Eighth graders also showed an increase in reading portfolio scores over a two-year period, going from 18% to 70% above grade level. This school was comprised of 48% English-language learners, with all students qualifying for free or reduced-price lunch. Frey credited the school's success in student literacy on the development of learning communities. Through detailed documentation, Frey connected learning experiences with academic gains.

Castle, Arends, and Rockwood (2008) compared student achievement at a professional development school with student achievement at a control school over a six-year period. They compared the percentage of students who met state standards on the Connecticut Mastery Test in reading, writing, and mathematics. They found that more students at the professional development school moved from an unsatisfactory achievement level to a proficient or mastery achievement level than students at the control school; however, they did not assess the statistical significance of these differences.

Teitel (2004) reported that a Kansas State University research study (Yahnke, Shroyer, Bietau, Hancock, & Bennett, 2003) identified a clear connection between student academic achievement and the level of PDS attainment. In the study, student achievement test scores in mathematics were tracked over multiple years. The PDS scores were compared to state averages and to each other based on length of time as a professional development school, self-assessment ratings aligned with the NCATE PDS standards, learning communities, and faculty engagement. According to Teitel, the researchers found a 19.0% gain in the oldest third of the professional

development schools as compared to a 0.7% gain in the newest professional development schools. The middle group of professional development
schools showed a 26.0% gain. The researchers discovered that the level of
faculty involvement was more important than the length of time a school
had been a professional development school. Schools reporting a high level
of faculty engagement showed a 23% gain over schools with low faculty involvement at 3%. The report also included a description of student academic achievement improvement in a low-performing, high-poverty school that
showed an annual gain of about 30%, which was triple the state average.

These studies and others (e.g., Cave & Brown, 2010; Creasy, 2005) suggest
that professional development schools can have a positive effect on student
achievement scores. Implementation of a professional development school
partnership is a complex undertaking that requires coordination among
many individuals and organizations, and modest student achievement increases may not be enough to convince policymakers, universities, school
systems, local communities, and teachers that a professional development
school intervention can be an effective educational intervention. However, a
professional development school implementation focused on collaboration,
reform, and renewal (Teitel, 1999) can create a learning environment that
supports the development of successful pre-service teachers and strengthens
the skills and knowledge of master teachers and university faculty members,
contributing to the professionalization of teachers, encouraging new teachers to remain committed to their callings as teachers, and creating a repu-
table cadre of talented individuals to serve in the nation's schools. The result
should be better learning experiences for all students.

REFERENCES

Abdal-Haqq, I. (1996). An information provider's perspective on the professional
development movement. *Contemporary Education, 67*(4), 237–239.
Abdal-Haqq, I. (1998). *Professional development schools: Weighing the evidence.* Thou-
sand Oaks, CA: Corwin Press.
Arends, R., & Winitzsky, N. (1996). Program structures and learning to teach. In
F. B. Murray (Ed.), *The teacher educator's handbook: Building a base for the prepara-
tion of teachers.* San Francisco: Jossey-Bass.
Book, C. L. (1996). Professional development schools. In J. Sikula, T. Buttery, &
E. Guyton (Eds.), *Handbook of research on teacher education* (2nd ed., pp. 194–
210). New York: Macmillan.
Campoy, R. W. (2000). *A professional development school partnership: Conflict and col-
laboration.* Westport, CT: Bergin & Garvey.
Carnegie Forum on Education and Economy. (1986). *A nation prepared: Teachers for
the 21st Century.* New York: Author.

Carnegie Foundation for the Advancement of Teaching. (1920). *15th annual report of the President and Treasurer.* New York: Author.

Castle, S., Arends, R. L., & Rockwood, K. D. (2008). Student learning in a professional development school and a control school. *The Professional Educator, 32*(1), 1–15.

Cave, A., & Brown, C. W. (2010). When learning is at stake: Exploration of the role of teacher training and professional development schools on elementary students' math achievement. *National Forum of Teacher Education Journal, 20*(3), 1–21.

Clark, R. W. (1999). *Effective professional development schools.* San Francisco: Jossey-Bass.

Cook, T. D. (2002). Randomized experiments in education: Why are they so rare? *Educational Evaluation and Policy Analysis, 24*(3), 175–199.

Creasy, K. (2005). *The effects of a professional development school program on student achievement as measured by the Iowa Test of Basic Skills, teacher perceptions of school climate, and pre-service teacher reflections.* Unpublished doctoral dissertation. The University of Akron, OH.

Darling-Hammond, L. (1992). Teaching and knowledge: Policy issues posed by alternate certification for teachers. *Peabody Journal of Education, 67*(3), 123–154.

Darling-Hammond, L. (2000). How teacher education matters. *Journal of Teacher Education, 51*(3), 166–173.

Darling-Hammond, L. (2005). *Professional development schools: Schools for developing a profession.* New York: Teachers College Press.

Darling-Hammond, L. (2006). Constructing 21st century teacher education. *Journal of Teacher Education, 57*(3), 300–314.

Dewey, J. (1896). The university school. *University Record, 5,* 417–442.

Dixon, P. L., & Ishler, R. (1992). Acceptable approaches to alternative certification. *Teacher Education and Practice, 8*(1), 29–35.

Flexner, A. (1914). *Medical education in the United States and Canada: A report to the Carnegie Foundation for the advancement of teaching.* New York: Carnegie Foundation for the Advancement of Teaching.

Fowler, R. C. (2009). Educators without borders: Addressing New England's teacher shortages. *New England Journal of Higher Education, Summer,* 10–11.

Frasier, C. M. (1994). Two education reform trains: Standards/assessment and simultaneous renewal. *Record in Educational Leadership, 14*(2), 15–17.

Frey, N. (2002). Literacy achievement in an urban middle-level professional development school: A learning community at work. *Reading Improvement. 39*(1), 3–13.

Fuhrman, S. (1999). *The new accountability.* Philadelphia: Consortium for Policy Research in Education.

Fulton, K., Yoon, I., & Lee, C. (2005, August). *Induction into learning communities.* National Commission on Teaching and America's Future. Retrieved from http://www.nctaf.org/documents/nctaf/NCTAF_Induction_Paper_2005.pdf

Georgia Partnership for Excellence in Education. (2006). Gap analysis: Georgia's unfinished business in teacher quality. Retrieved from http://www/gpee/org

Gill, B., & Hove, A. (2000). *The Benedum collaborative model of teacher education: A preliminary study.* Pittsburg: Rand Education.

Goodlad, J. I. (1994). The National Network for Educational Renewal. *Phi Delta Kappan, 75*(8), 632–639.

Grissmer, D., & Kirby, S. N. (1987). *Teacher attrition: The uphill climb to staff the nation's schools.* Santa Monica, CA: The RAND Corporation, R-3512-CSTP.

Guarino, C.M., Santibanez, L., Daley, G. (2006). Teacher recruitment and retention: A review of the recent empirical literature. *Review of Educational Research, 76*(2), 173–208.

Hallinan, M. T., & Khmelkov, V. T. (2001). Recent developments in teacher education in the United States of American. *Journal of Education for Teaching, 27*(2), 175–185.

Hoffman, N. E., Reed, W. M., & Rosenbluth, G. S. (1997). In N. E. Hoffman, W. M. Reed, & G. S. Rosenbluth (Eds.), *Lessons from restructuring experiences: Stories of change in professional development schools* (pp. 1–6). Albany: State University of New York Press.

Holmes Group. (1986). *Tomorrow's teachers: A report of the Holmes Group.* East Lansing, MI: Author.

Holmes Group. (1990). *State of principles: Tomorrow's schools: Principles for the design of professional development schools.* East Lansing, MI: Author.

Holmes Group. (1995). *Tomorrow's schools of education.* East Lansing, MI: Author.

Houston, W. R., Clay, D., Hollis, L. Y., Ligons, C., Roff, L., & Lopez, N. (1995). *Strength through diversity: Houston consortium for professional development and technology centers.* (ERIC Document Reproduction Service No. ED 404303)

Houston, W. R., Hollis, L. Y., Clay, D., Ligons, C. M., & Roff, L. (1999). Effects of collaboration on urban teacher education programs and professional development schools. In D. M. Byrd & J. McIntyre (Eds.), *Research on Professional Development Schools: Teacher Education Yearbook VII* (pp. 6–28). Thousand Oaks, CA: Corwin Press, Inc.

Imig, D., & Imig, S. (2005, September/October). The learned report on teacher education: A vision delayed. *Change Magazine* [online].

Judge, H., Carriendo, R., & Johnson, S. M. (1995). *Professional development schools and MSU: The report of the 1995 review.* Michigan State University College of Education. Retrieved from http://edweb3.educ.msu.edu/pds/archive.html

Johnson, S. & Birkeland, S. (2003). Pursuing a "sense of success": New teachers explain their career decisions. *American Educational Research Journal, 40*(3), 581–617.

Knight, S. L., Wiseman, D. L., & Cooner, D. (2000). Using collaborative teacher research to determine the impact of professional development school activities on elementary students' math and writing outcomes. *Journal of Teacher Education, 51*(1), 26–38.

Levin, M. (Ed.). (1992). *Professional practice schools: Linking teacher education and school reform.* Teachers College Press: New York.

Levin, M., & Churins, E. J. (1999). Designing standards that empower professional development schools. *Peabody Journal of Education, 74*(3&4), 178–208.

McDonnell, L. (2004). *Politics, persuasion and educational testing.* Cambridge, MA: Harvard University Press.

National Commission on Excellence in Education. (1992). *A nation at risk: The full account.* Portland, OR: USA Research, Inc. (Original work published in 1984).

National Council for Accreditation of Teacher Education. (2001). *Standards for professional development schools.* Washington, DC: Author.

Neapolitan, J. E., & Scott, C. (2004). The NCATE Professional Development School Standards Field Test Project. In J. E. Neapolitan, T. D. Proffitt, C. L. Wittman, & T. R. Berkeley (Eds.), *Traditions, standards, and transformations: A model for professional development school networks*. New York: Peter Lang.

Newman, J. W. (2006). *America's teachers: An introduction to education*. New York: Pearson.

No Child Left Behind Act. 20 U.S.C. § 6301. (2001).

Osguthorpe, R. T., Harris, R. C., Harris, M. F., & Black, S. (1995). Appendix: National Network for Educational Renewal site descriptions. In R. T. Osguthorpe, R. C. Harris, J. F. Harris, & S. Black (Eds.), *Partner Schools: Centers for Educational Renewal* (pp. 283–310). San Francisco: Jossey-Bass.

Petrie, H. G. (Ed.). (1995). *Professionalization, partnership, and power: Building professional development schools*. Albany: State University of New York Press.

Pine, G. J. (2003). Making a differences: A professional development school's impact on student learning. In D. L. Wiseman & S. L. Knight (Eds.), *Linking school-university collaboration and K–12 student outcomes*. Washington, DC: AACTE Publications.

Pugach, M. C., & Johnson, L. J. (2002). *Collaborative practitioners, collaborative schools*. Denver, CO: Love Publishing Company.

Riehl, C. (2006). Feeling better: A comparison of medical research and education research. *Educational Researcher, 35*(5), 24–29.

Sewell, T. E., Shapiro, J. P., Ducett, J. P., & Stanford, J. S. (1995). Professional development schools in the inner city: Policy implications for school-university collaboration. In H. G. Petrie (Ed.), *Professionalization, partnership, and power: Building professional development schools* (p. 179–198). Albany: State University of New York Press.

Slavin, R. E. (2004). Education research can and must address "what works" questions. *Educational Researcher, 33*(1), 27–28.

Stafford, D., & Shaughnessy, M. F. (2006). An interview with Delia Stafford about alternative certification. *North American Journal of Psychology, 8*(3), 497–502.

Stallings, J. A., & Kowalski, T. (1990). Research on professional development schools. In W. R. Houston (Ed.), *Handbook of research on teacher education* (pp. 251–263). New York: Macmillan.

Stoddart, T. (1993). The professional development school: Building bridges between cultures. Educational Policy 7, 5–23.

Teitel, L. (1999). Looking toward the future by understanding the past: The historical context of professional development schools. *Peabody Journal of Education, 74*(3 & 4), 6–20.

Teitel, L. (2001a). *How professional development schools make a difference: A review of research*. Washington, DC: National Council for Accreditation of Teacher Education.

Teitel, L. (2001b). An assessment framework for professional development schools. *Journal of Teacher Education, 52*(1), 57–71.

Teitel, L. (2004) *How professional development schools make a difference: A review of research*. Washington, DC: National Council for Accreditation of Teacher Education.

Trachtman, R. (1996). The NCATE professional development schools study: A survey of 28 sites. Unpublished manuscript. (Available from Professional Development School Standards Project, National Council for Accreditation of Teacher Education, Washington, DC 20036).

Williams, R. (1993). A professional development school initiative: Indiana State University story. *Contemporary Education, 64*(4), 210–214.

Wiseman, D. L., & Cooner, D. (1996). Discovering the power of collaboration. *Teacher Education and Practice, 12*(1), 18–28.

Wright, D. P., McKibbon, M., & Walton, P. (1987). *The effectiveness of the teacher trainee program: An alternate route into teaching in California.* Sacramento, CA: California Commission on Teacher Credentialing.

Yahnke, S., Shroyer, G., Bietau, L., Hancock, M., & Bennett, A. (2005). Collaborating to renew and reform K–16 education. In L. Darling-Hammond (Ed.), *Professional development schools: Schools for developing a profession* (pp. 21–36). New York, NY: Teacher College Press

Zeichner, K. (1992). Rethinking the practicum in the professional development school partnership. *Journal of Teacher Education, 43*(4), 296–307.

CHAPTER 3

THE WORK AND INSIGHTS OF PROFESSIONAL DEVELOPMENT SCHOOL BOUNDARY SPANNERS IN CLINICAL TEACHER EDUCATION

Joyce E. Many, Teresa Fisher, Dee Taylor, and Gwen Benson
Georgia State University

The key to improving education and clinical teacher education partnerships is to facilitate the mutual understanding of participants involved and to find strategies to bridge differences. Educators involved in clinical preparation in school partnerships and professional development schools (PDS) need resources to promote authentic collaboration, and the concept of a *boundary spanner* is such a tool. Stevens (1999) describes the PDS boundary spanner as one who commutes both figuratively and in reality across public school and university boundaries. Professional development schools consist of collaborations across institutions whose missions, organizational

Clinical Teacher Education, pages 33–53
Copyright © 2011 by Information Age Publishing
All rights of reproduction in any form reserved.

structures, and cultures are distinct and which, in some ways, may conflict (Sandholtz & Finan, 1990). Partners in PDS schools may encounter hidden barriers and mismatched perspectives because of differing emphases across contexts (Stevens, 1999). For this reason, we have found the work and insights of boundary spanners to be particularly beneficial in the creation and operation of a PDS network.

The concept of boundary spanner has its foundation in organizational theory, where such individuals are seen as providing important links between organizations and the environments in which they are situated (White & Dozier, 1992). A boundary spanner's role is to relay information from outside the environment to key decision makers within the organization. Because of a boundary spanner's links to outsiders, he/she can stimulate reflection and creativity, can help to negotiate goals in light of the needs of external audiences, and can bring new meanings to the surface by interpreting behaviors, events, people, and information for both internal and external audiences (Aldridge & Herker, 1977; White et al., 1992). Boundary spanners essentially speak the languages of both contexts and are able to translate across boundary lines.

In schools, boundary spanners bridge discourses, provide cultural guidance, and act as change agents (Buxton, Carlone, & Carlone, 2005). Such individuals have been found to play crucial roles in understanding differing perspectives and in creating and maintaining school-university partnerships (Collay, 1995; Sandholtz et al., 1990). Because their knowledge and experiences cross the borders of schools and academia, they are able to interpret, communicate, and extend traditional relations (Stevens, 1999).

In our PDS network, we have a growing number of university-based and school-based boundary spanners. Because their knowledge and expertise spans across both contexts, these individuals are able to provide us with an enhanced understanding and appreciation for the complexity of our partnership. In this chapter, we explore the diverse roles of boundary spanners which have evolved across the course of our collaboration, and then we discuss what we see as the importance of boundary spanners to clinical teacher education partnerships.

OUR BOUNDARY SPANNERS' STORIES

The four stories we share in this section focus on (a) a professional development school (PDS) intern who became a PDS teacher, (b) a PDS teacher who became an Urban Teaching Fellow and then a clinical faculty member in our university teacher education programs, (c) a university graduate research assistant who assumed the responsibilities of research administrator in a school system, and (d) a school system administrator who crossed the boundary to the university to direct the entire PDS network's grant-supported initiatives. By listening to the voices of these boundary spanners, we begin to understand the unique contributions participants from each context can bring to the creation of a new space which bridges our educational communities.

From Serving as an Intern to Working as PDS Teacher: Shari's Story

To understand the boundary spanner role from the perspective of an individual who had interned in a PDS during her teacher preparation program and who then was hired to be a teacher at that same school, we would like share Shari's story. Shari is a second year kindergarten teacher at one of the inner-city schools in our PDS network. She received her undergraduate degree in our early childhood education program and then returned to our university to enroll in an Urban Teacher Leadership program for her master's degree. A young, energetic, African American, Shari is extraordinarily informative regarding her experiences and how her varying roles within a PDS site have impacted her growth as an educator.

In spite of the fact that she is only a second year teacher, Shari was nominated by both the professors and her school principal as a potentially excellent mentor for practicum students. Shari explains that they "understood that I can offer the people coming from the university a little bit of a different perspective than a veteran teacher or a beginning teacher who has never been in a PDS-type program." In her first two years, Shari has already worked with two interns. Shari is enthusiastic about the numbers of interns at her school, noting, "it is nothing to see a new face."

Shari believes the fact that she has only recently completed her undergraduate degree makes her more approachable to many of the interns. She says, it's not like I have been teaching for 30 years...I think when they see me and they see someone who's only in their second year but actually has developed a routine, has developed strategies to use with the kids that are effective, I think that helps them." She observed that when interacting with her, interns are not as scared to admit that they don't know something or to ask questions like, 'How are you able to get all these things in the room? Did you have to buy everything?" Both Shari's age and her recent experiences in the same clinical teacher preparation program seem to help interns feel comfortable in confiding in her. She continued "some of them will come from other people's classrooms and they'll come in or buddy up and bring each other down to my room and they'll ask those questions that I think sometimes you're scared [to ask]." Shari thinks that interns find her particularly approachable as she is "still at year two, and its [someone] realistic to look to for examples and for situations that may occur when they start teaching."

Shari also remarked that having an intern in her kindergarten classroom has been helpful to her own teaching practices. She stressed that her interns "continuously brought things from [the university]" which helped her as "so many new things had been coming out in education" even in the short time since she had been out of school. She also recognized that interns are beneficial to her students because it allows the children to have access to three educators: herself, her paraprofessional, and the intern. She stated, "our classrooms are already busting at the seams at 20 children" and that "interns are another set of eyes, and [they] hear things that you as a teacher may not hear or see—someone who may be having difficulties that they can bring to your attention." In her opinion, interns are able to plan fantastic lessons that are fun and meaningful for her students and "really get the children excited about learning." Shari's kindergarten students "really embrace the idea that it's another teacher. And I really help them understand that [the interns are] not a teacher like myself, but they're getting ready to be a teacher like me so it's even better because you guys are teaching them." Having an intern also helps her own practice, as Shari finds that she is always asking her interns about new research. In addition, because her classroom is often visited by the supervisors of interns (her former professors), Shari also has continual access to former mentors who continue to give suggestions and advice. According to Shari, "It is just great to have another person come in."

Reflecting on her experiences as a PDS boundary spanner, Shari emphasized three major ways that her background as a PDS intern and student teacher has impacted her work as a mentor teacher: (a) in understanding the pre-service teachers' roles as university students and as interns, (b) in supporting interns as they increase their engagement in classroom instruction, and (c) in scaffolding interns as they work to connect the theories they are learning in the university setting with the pedagogical implementations in actual classrooms.

The first way Shari felt her position as a boundary spanner aided her as a mentor teacher was in her ability to understand the multiple roles that pre-service teachers must juggle in their lives as university students and as teaching interns. Shari explains that it is often "hard for other teachers to . . . comprehend" an intern's role and to understand that "they're not only working with you, but they also have a full load" of coursework. She also contrasts the responsibilities of interns in initial field experiences with those involved in full time clinical practice, explaining, a "cooperating teacher may expect [an intern] to do the duties of a student teacher" not "understanding the stages that the intern goes through in the program." The importance of understanding the out of classroom rigor of her interns' lives makes Shari particularly attentive to her interns. She explains that even when her interns have left her classroom context she emails them just to say,

> how's the workload going? Because they need to know it's not a business in education...Even though there's money behind it, it's not a business because you're actually dealing with real people. And those real people are not only the kids, but also the teachers that teach those kids.

Her experiences as a student in the program have made her a particularly empathetic and supportive mentor teacher for the interns she has hosted in her classroom.

A second way being a boundary spanner helps Shari bring unique perspectives to her work as a cooperating teacher is evident when she talks about her supervision of interns. Shari notes that she does approach mentoring differently as a result of her in-depth knowledge of the clinical teacher preparation program. "Because I have been through it...I know what [an intern] should be doing in week three because I know to look at the calendar and say, 'Hey, can you come in and do a "routine task" because you're at week three [in your internship responsibilities] and you haven't gotten to that point yet.'" She also remembers how important it is that her interns feel "comfortable in the classroom setting because it wasn't too long ago for me that I was right there in their position." As a result, Shari supports the interns by encouraging them to take on leadership roles in her classroom. From her past experience, she knows how hard it is for interns to speak up and ask to teach a lesson when they are observing their mentor teacher doing a great job with the students. She handles her interns' initial discomfort by saying something like "I'm teaching this great lesson, how about we do small groups together?" to encourage the interns to become more engaged in classroom instruction. In such ways, Shari gradually provides interns with responsibilities and opportunities to facilitate student learning.

In these ways, Shari's familiarity with the program and the expectations associated with the internship enables her to be an excellent guide and resource for her interns. In addition, being a boundary spanner helps Shari also understand the importance of emphasizing connections between theory and practice. She explicitly assists the interns in making connections between the content they learn in the university classes and the actual practices in the daily life of a classroom teacher. She clarifies that she often asks,

> "what are you guys doing in class? How can you really make this match?" Because sometimes they don't see the gray area, they just see black and white, [the university] and the elementary school that I'm at. They don't actually see the common ground that they can come to.... I remember feeling like what we do [at the university] is great but I don't see it in the classroom. I would say,

'gosh they had great guided reading they had great phonics skills that they taught us. And when we're in the classroom we don't see that as much' . . . So I try to even point out, 'Look, remember when you guys learned about literacy labs? Look we have literacy labs around the classroom.' and they just have to see it. They're looking for it to have the plain, written out signs 'Literacy Labs.' So when you show them that the things that they are learning are real and not so text-book like it helps them understand, 'Hey look! What I'm doing here is not just fairy tale, it is reality!'

By helping the students connect what they are learning to what they are seeing, Shari noted that she is helping them learn how to be the type of teachers they hope to be.

She says she thinks it is very important to help future teachers understand that there are required approaches mandated in some schools and that they may have to learn how to retain "the best of the best" strategies and pedagogical orientations from their coursework and think of ways to draw on that information within educational reforms they may experience in schools. Shari elaborated on what she believes interns need to understand,

> You're going to go into an educational system that may not mirror what you learned at [the university] but you still stay with those strategies, stay with those techniques, stay with those engaging activities, hands-on types of learning skills because your classroom cannot be a reform model. Your classroom has to work for your students. And if that model or program isn't working for your students, you're going to have to put more of your own energy into it.

Shari particularly emphasizes the need to prepare teachers to work in clinical settings where they have to be mindful of standardized testing or scripted curriculum. She recognizes that while teacher candidates need to work within those mandates, they should "still teach, not just read a book [teaching script] all day." As a result, within the context of the scripted curriculum in her school, Shari demonstrates to her interns how to use excellent strategies by adapting, adding to, and supplementing the aspects of curriculum that she is not able to change. She helps her interns mediate between the ideal and the actual, the "perfect classroom strategies" they read about in their classes and her actual classroom where great teaching and theory is informing practice in spite of multiple mandates. To Shari, clinical teacher preparation programs in PDS schools must prepare educators "who are able to work under the pressure of having all of these mandates and still have students excel, rather than the teacher who goes in there and just falls into the regiment of what the system has set up." As a result, she exhorts her interns to be committed to "real teaching" and helps her pre-service teachers find their way to strike that balance in the midst of challenging educational policies.

Reflecting on her experiences as a boundary spanner, Shari was able to offer recommendations for how to improve the professional development school collaborative. Shari feels that the partnership could be strengthened by creating a position for a full time liaison who is a teacher from the school system. While each of the current PDS schools working within this university network has an identified PDS school coordinator, most are administrators or curriculum specialists within the school. Shari emphasized the need for a liaison who does not serve in an evaluative or administrative role at the school. She believes that reconceptualizing the liaison position and filling that position with a former classroom teacher would enable liaisons to really dedicate all of their time to building PDS relationships, supporting all involved and strengthening the partnership in ways that are meaningful and site specific. She envisions this individual as an accomplished teacher leader who is able to enter other classrooms, acting as kind of a coach, finding out what types of supports the teachers need, pulling resources, modeling and collaborating with them. Such an individual could observe all interns and student teachers, serve as a collaborator and resource, and provide interns with continuity across their field experiences. In addition, the person in this role should develop in-service teachers' ability to assist, scaffold, and supervise interns and student teachers and could also provide a channel for clear communication between the teachers and the university.

From Working as a PDS Teacher to Becoming an Urban Graduate Teaching Fellow: Terry's Story

Our second boundary spanner and coauthor of this chapter, Teresa Fisher (Terry), began working at the university as an Urban Graduate Teaching Fellow and is now a clinical faculty member at the university. Terry taught for five years in a Title One elementary school just outside the immediate perimeter of the city. She worked with newly arrived immigrant students in first and second grade to support their literacy and language development. During this time, the site was chosen to become a new professional development school with our institution.

As a teacher in a professional development school in the initial years of the collaboration, Terry participated in professional learning opportunities to further her understanding of language and literacy development, engaged in a research project which encouraged teacher input for change in the context of the school environment, and acted as a mentor and collaborating teacher for interns from the university. These experiences have shaped Terry's university work, commitments, engagement, and emphases in her current role as a boundary spanner. Her university-based work has encompassed the provision of professional learning opportunities for in-service educators, inquiry with teachers in PDS schools, and on-going support of interns and collaborating teachers in a teacher education program. She also has coordinated and worked to reshape two alternative certification programs in our university.

School-based professional development opportunities. Terry's experience working as a teacher in a PDS afforded her some unique learning opportunities. She attended speaking engagements when literacy scholars visited the university and was offered the opportunity to meet scholars in the field whose work informed her pedagogy. These opportunities made her feel like a respected professional. Participating in a continuing learning engagement provided by the university was significant, as it signified the commitment of university faculty to her knowledge base and improvement as an educator. She felt that the partnership was developing her expertise in ways that impacted her teaching and her students' learning.

As a classroom teacher working in a PDS, Terry worked closely with her colleagues, engaging in informal inquiry and reflecting upon teaching practices in order to meet the academic, linguistic, cognitive, and social needs of the ELLs in her classroom. The significance of learning with and from her teaching colleagues is evident as she described the value of collaborative educative practices and educators as communities of learners.

> It's not enough now to close your door and say 'What happens in my classroom stays in my classroom.' Our classrooms are affected by everything that our kids bring in and everything that they take out. We are not a little microcosm that is unaffected by the rest of the world and we can't act like we are. If we have somebody that we can reflect with and talk to, then we can trouble the commonplace [which] will exponentially improve our practice and the learning of our students.

Terry's involvement in this group of reflective practitioners significantly influenced her future practices in the university clinical teacher education context, where she worked to create and support reflective professional learning communities where members examined and improved upon their own practices.

One of Terry's initial responsibilities as a boundary spanner was to organize and implement ESOL and reading endorsement programs for practicing teachers in the PDS network. She worked to create a context in her work with teachers at PDS schools that facilitated the establishment of a community of supportive faculty that could be sustained at the school long after the endorsement process was over. Throughout these year long endorsements, strong relationships were built. Many of the PDS teachers conducted collaborative inquiry projects, case studies, and other types of participant action research to learn more about their students, their teaching practices, and the ways that they could more effectively advocate for their students.

The teachers in these courses often explained that they felt they were rarely treated as professionals and welcomed the opportunities to explore and develop their expertise through the coursework offered in connection to the university. From Terry's perspective, professional communities consisting of university and school faculty in long-term engagements "give teachers a place to ask...inquire...be troubled by and find potential solutions" to issues which concern them and their daily practices. She believes that the most effective professional development opportunities often consist of "teachers sitting down together, problematizing, [conducting] inquiry and figuring out what is causing the issues and how they can make a change." She further argues that this type of teacher led development is unlikely to occur without first "building relationships and creating a safe space for teachers to talk about and grapple with their practices." She thinks that it is imperative that university faculty "really consider the needs and feelings, experiences, questions, and ponderings of teachers."

The importance of building real and meaningful relationships between teachers and also with university faculty is a process that takes time and commitment on the part of all participants. Terry finds herself constantly discussing the role of relationships as she crosses the boundary and stated, "We need to continue to think through the relationships that we're building and give them the time and space that they need, so everybody has a space where they can live and learn and grow with confidence."

Research in PDS initiatives. While a classroom teacher, Terry participated in a research project examining school climate and teacher attrition that was initiated due to teacher concern and facilitated by the PDS faculty liaison to her school. This opportunity to be a voice for change in the school context was a meaningful opportunity for Terry and for many of her colleagues. She viewed this experience as an opportunity for teachers to have a say in the future of the school and explained that "talking about, thinking about, and envisioning potential solutions instead of just complaining in our grade level meetings" was meaningful. She further explained that the ability of the university to bring forward a research agenda proposed by the teachers and the staff in order to understand a problem that they wanted addressed and solved "was so important, valuable, and empowering to many of the teachers in the school."

Terry's appreciation for the way in which research could open up opportunities for teachers' voices to be heard continued as she took on her new responsibilities at the university. Her interest in establishing collaborative relationships across the university and PDS practices, as well as her sensitivity for the necessity of teachers' voice in the direction of their work, professional development, and partnership with the university was also apparent in an action research project that was a second focus of Terry's boundary spanner work. She was particularly interested in understanding the perspectives of teachers who had worked with our graduate-level ESOL initial teacher preparation program, and helping the university use teachers' feedback to consider opportunities for programmatic change in clinical teacher preparation and in-service teacher support.

In order to gather information, Terry and one of her colleagues met with small groups of collaborating teachers in multiple PDS settings to determine teacher perceptions, beliefs and suggestions about the PDS relationship. Teachers expressed multiple and varied needs for their own professional development that they hoped the university could help provide. There were individuals who thought that they received very little out of the PDS relationship and that they were not treated as equal partners in the clinical preparation of teachers. Teachers' statements also clearly indicated that they wanted to have more voice and collaboration with university supervisors in the training of pre-service teachers. PDS teachers believed they had much to contribute to the development of clinical teacher education programs but did not feel that they had a real forum in which to share their contributions with the faculty.

> We talked to collaborating teachers to figure out how we can improve the program and how we can make the collaboration better. It was really informative about the lines of communication that we need to open. I think that my experiences as a collaborative teacher drove that [action research] and [it] has driven my hopes, goals, aspirations, and values for the program.

Terry found that without a more collaborative, respectful and mutually beneficial alliance, a PDS can feel to the teachers as "just another thing to go through and check off." She believes that PDS relationships have always been great in theory, but that the collaborative processes often fall short in the implementation stage, as too often true collaboration is not achieved and teachers in the schools rarely have real voice, choice, or find real benefit in the partnership.

Clinical teacher preparation in PDS schools. As a first- and second-grade teacher in a PDS, Terry supervised student interns and was able to reflect, both with her interns and with her colleagues hosting other interns, about the practices, policies, and procedures that were in place and how they could be reframed to provide more input from collaborative teachers. In thinking about her early experiences as a PDS mentor teacher, Terry explained:

> I have no recollection of the supervisors who came into my classroom to supervise interns. I don't remember any type of real collaboration occurring. My insight and ideas were not really asked for or integrated into the student's plan. Instead, [the interns] were pulled out of my class to have a debriefing and I had little opportunity for... collaboration with the faculty. As it occurred, the placements were meaningful to the interns and a good experi-

ence for me to practice articulating the situated knowledge and application of theory into practice. However, they were not an opportunity to collaborate, build a relationship, or engage with faculty in any meaningful way.

After Terry's second year as an urban teaching fellow at the university, Terry became the program coordinator of the ESOL initial teacher certification program. In that capacity she had a variety of responsibilities including instructing classes, coordinating internship and student teaching placements, supervising student teachers, and building and maintaining relationships with schools and administration to ensure future relationships. Again, her experiences spanning both sides of the boundary allowed her to bring a unique set of perspectives to the PDS relationship.

As a university faculty member, Terry places tremendous value in building relationships with the mentor teachers and serving as a resource for them. Recognizing her strong feelings in this area, she notes that her orientation toward supervision of student teachers differs from many of her colleagues. Where other supervisors focus on being a support for the intern, Terry conceptualizes her role as being a supportive resource to both the intern and the mentor teacher. She believes that,

> It is very important, as the university supervisor, that I create relationships with the collaborating teachers. I'm there to serve as an assistant and a conversation partner to the collaborating teacher as well, so they become used to seeing me as a resource, as somebody [who] comes in and has something to offer and things to share, not as an intimidating presence.

Terry expressed frustration that in many of the schools where she worked as a supervisor and did not have established relationships, she had much more difficulty acting as a resource to the collaborative teachers "because [supervising teachers] don't know if they can really talk to you. They don't know who you're going to go back to and report to." She contrasts that experience with the potentiality of collaborating with the teachers she worked with for over a year in the endorsements or her colleagues at the PDS where she taught for five years. It was not necessary in those contexts to build trusting and collaborative relationships, as those relationships had been established over a long period of time. In those contexts where teacher/university faculty relationships were strong, the teachers could see the pedagogical and professional advantage to having a university faculty person as a resource and partner in reflection. Without those strong relationships, the full potentiality of partnering with and supporting in-service teachers is rarely actualized.

> If we don't build upon the relationships we have and create the spaces where we can be a resource to cooperating teachers, then our interns are not going

to have the type of pre-service experiences they need to have. They're going to go in and have frustrated cooperating teachers to whom this is just another thing, who don't feel like they're going to get anything out of this and who are down-trodden because of the general circumstances of the system. This is a great potentiality. The challenge is moving from what-is to what could be.

In spite of the complexity of building trusting relationships in the context of a teacher's classroom, Terry views serving as a collaborative resource for both student teacher and mentor teacher as an essential, yet difficult aspect of clinical teacher education partnerships that need to be developed. She stated,

> It's time for us to have good relationships with schools... where we are all developing professionally and creating spaces that are healthy and open. It's important that [our interns] have positive models that are encouraging and supportive and who care about being teachers and care about the students that they serve. And that is, I believe, why teachers go into education in the first place. This process will also enable partner schools to help our interns develop professionally because the period of student teaching and internship is where they enact the theory and method they have studied in their coursework. If everyone involved in the PDS network works together to create a collaborative and mutually beneficial environment... I think that we can really change the education that the children are receiving, the training that pre-service teachers are getting, and the practice of current teachers.

Terry believes that PDS relationships hold great potentialities for teaching, clinical teacher preparation, and student learning. She states:

> I think if [PDS is] done well, and we have our interns in schools that are supportive, with in-service teachers that are ready, willing, able and excited to collaborate, then this is the model that we should all be moving toward. If we pick a school and we go into it and their role is just to have our interns come in, that's not the professional development school model. That is the old school model. In education we are way too good at not changing our practice but changing the acronyms. If we do PDS, more than just giving it the name and giving it the lip service, if we actually do it, that is going to impact the lives of the students that we serve, the future teaching of the teachers who we train, and also the current practice of the teachers who are already affecting students' lives.

Terry firmly believes that the PDS network must be mutually beneficial, collaboratively envisioned and enacted, and frequently examined by those engaged in the relationship. This creates a partnership which develops all professionals. Fundamentally, Terry believes that creating communities of teachers and learners and providing personally and contextually relevant in-service and pre-service teacher development based on reflection will significantly increase teacher efficacy and support student success.

From Being a University Graduate Research Assistant to Serving as a System Research Administrator: Carol's Story

Our third boundary spanner story focuses on the experiences of Carol, a research specialist for one of the systems in our PDS network. Carol began her PDS involvement as a graduate student working as an assistant to the director of research and evaluation for our PDS project. In this role, she worked on the organization of data and keeping track of who was collecting data, from which school system and site. Carol later became involved in data analysis and assisted in fine tuning some of the constructed response questions used to collect information on student achievement. While she still keeps in regular communication with the university director of research and evaluation and with research coordinators, she has found it interesting to see what is happening in the PDS network from a school district's perspective. In her new position she notes she is "using what I learned in theory, what I know in theory and putting it into practice myself."

In Carol's new role, she has broader responsibilities as a research administrator than just the PDS network's initiatives. However, she notes, "because I started out [at the university] and really being involved from the inside or involved intimately with the PDS as far as the data, it made me appreciate the project more and it made me see the importance of having the school systems involved in their role." Carol draws on that knowledge as she interacts with decision makers who may have less appreciation for the move to professional development school relationships. She explains, "I've been responsible for communicating the importance of the PDS to those key players there who perhaps did not realize the importance of this project. I've been able to communicate its importance and encourage the school system to continue with this project." In such ways, Carol's personal knowledge and experience from the university's perspective with the PDS network allows her to help others within the school system administration understand the value of the school-university partnership.

Carol believes that the overall movement in clinical teacher education towards preparing teachers in professional development schools is excellent. She notes, "I think that more universities need to take an active role in shaping teachers to go out into the school systems and teach. Universities across the United States need to take a more active role with the various districts that fall on their jurisdictions or area and work more collaboratively with them. I think it's a great thing." At the same time, from a research and evaluation perspective Carol realizes the complexities of establishing the impact of the initiative itself. She believes the PDS work is effective but notes that "it's not always easy to measure it because very often in the schools there are other competing programs, so sometimes its hard to pin-point which one is, or the combination of programs, is contributing to increased student achievement, which is what we all want." However, she does believe that from her vantage as a boundary spanner, the PDS relationship has been very effective.

From School System Administrator to PDS Director: Dee's Story

Dee Taylor (coauthor of this chapter) has been the project director for the two major PDS grants which have supported the development and expansion of our PDS network. Previously, she was the executive director for professional learning in the school system of one of the PDS district partners. In that role, she was responsible for all of the professional development for professional staff and auxiliary staff in the district as well as establishing partnerships with universities and others for training to be conducted in the district. She was also very heavily involved in several grants which provided induction support for teachers, professional learning for veteran teachers, and development for all auxiliary support staff. In that capacity she was involved with mini-partnership initiatives that included partnering with our institution to provide a reading endorsement, and partnering with other institutions to provide leadership endorsements and training for aspiring administrators. In this capacity she was able to forge connections with our institution and bring her county into the PDS movement. She had participated in this type of collaboration for a long time, had seen its effectiveness in her district, and was eager to engage her county in clinical teacher education partnerships through the PDS initiative. Professional development schools research and the professional development key objectives to increase student achievement and retain teachers spoke to her passions. The opportunity to become the project director seemed like a natural step for her since she was already well connected in two of the partnership districts and could help "stand in the gap."

According to Dee, we need to "build bridges" so we understand the "driving forces on each side." The schools need to understand the need that professors have to conduct research and that such research is intended to directly benefit their schools, teachers, and students, and is often closely aligned to aspects of their school improvement plans. She also works to help schools understand that the university is not all theory but is also filled with excellent practitioners. At the same time, Dee stressed that the university must be aware of the "day to day operations, mandates, and the amount of pressure that public schools are particularly under to reach such things as AYP and all of the assessment that has to be prepared for." Dee pointed out, however, that "sometimes it's not as easy to collaborate." Dee underscored,

> respecting and valuing the goals on each side is essential to building the bridges, which is what I see as one of the most meaningful and satisfying aspects of my work. I am able to advocate for each side and I am able to inform the leadership on both sides. I am valued by both sides because of my longitudinal engagement with teacher development, curriculum and instruction.

Because of her vantage point Dee was also able to notice ways that we can continue to improve. She notes, "Professors could spend more time in the PDS schools, supporting pre-service teachers, cooperating teachers, administrators, and assistant principals and also learning about the current practices and contexts of schools, and participating in action research." She is encouraged about the shift in some degree programs to move to year-long internships which Dee believes will facilitate this type of longitudinal commitment. Overall, these improvements will enhance the clinical teacher education partnerships. She stressed,

> So the PDS, all of the design inquiry, the research-based pieces, the extended internships, more professional development time for professors to be in school to support new teachers, more support for growing administrators of PDS schools, and all of those that began with our initial initiatives will continue to strengthen our partnerships.

Dee thinks that the PDS initiative has been largely effective although all of the ways of measuring the effectiveness cannot always be quantified in terms of standardized test scores. From her vantage point she sees several things that have been particularly effective. She believes that the partnership has produced clarity about the different roles and responsibilities of both the university and the public schools. Professors have a clearer understanding of what goes on in schools and schools more clearly understand teacher preparation at the university. She also thinks the PDS relationship has fostered inquiry-based projects that benefit professors while they improve schools and classroom instruction. Professional development pathways for PDS participants have provided many opportunities to in-service teachers to earn additional credentials such as alternative certifications, and endorsements in ESOL, reading, mathematics, teacher support specialist and leadership trainings. Partner schools have also received a great deal of financial support that they have been able to use for consultants and professional development opportunities to help achieve AYP and other student achievement initiatives. These were significant benefits to PDS schools, which were neither top-down nor university driven activities, but rather were collaboratively constructed based on the unique needs of the school. Dee stated that the grant has been beneficial to school partners in a range of ways, specifically through

> recruiting and retaining teachers and improving student achievement. I think the meaning of the activities that the PDS grant has been involved in, such as the assessment, has informed instruction, has given information about what teachers need and want for professional development, and has identified some curricular gaps and strengths that can inform the instructional teams as they prepare for the state-mandated tests. These are really substantive ways that the grant has helped.

As we ended our first grant funded initiative and began the process of seeking additional federal funding, Dee had several recommendations that she felt needed to be considered. First, she felt it was important that we worked for clarity about what we were really looking for in a PDS school and that we should include an application process to ensure that our partner schools were fully invested in the collaboration. Second, she noted that we needed to be proactive and have components of our grant that consider the fact that there will be changes at the superintendent, principal, curriculum, and professorial levels and that we needed to consider how to be proactive and responsive as we adjusted to those changes. She believed that professors needed a type of front end orientation so they knew from the beginning the amount of time they were committing to and to ensure understanding about the meaning of school improvement processes and practices. She also encouraged the inclusion of longer internship periods, more emphasis on administrators, and a strategic emphasis on the types of support that administrators need to provide in PDS. She stated,

> We need to make sure that people are clear on what research means. We have been very fortunate to have anchor action research and that's been a very positive aspect [of the PDS network grant] but I think clarification on both sides of the partnership would be very important. I think that we need to be aggressive about ... projects that are going to serve. I think that we need to be real clear about publications that provide opportunities for co-publications [between school and university based faculty]. I think that's a value for both the school-based side and certainly the university side. I'd like to see us continue to support professional development opportunities for people to go to conferences that really serve the PDS initiative. I would like to see that continue as well.

As we wrote our proposal for our second federally funded grant and as we now begin to implement this grant, these principles have guided our thoughts and our practices.

THE IMPORTANCE OF BOUNDARY SPANNERS:
CROSSING CONTEXTS AND BUILDING BRIDGES

We believe listening to the voices of various types of boundary spanners who traverse the borders between universities and public schools is crucial to the development of effective clinical teacher education partnerships. These boundary spanners bring strong background knowledge and skills to the university and play important roles in designing and developing clinical teacher education partnerships in a range of ways. Strong connections to their prior experiences supported these boundary spanners in their work to (a) build, maintain, and strengthen relationships; (b) navigate across contexts while utilizing prior experiences and expertise; and (c) envision and bring into being meaningful change and authentically collaborative partnerships.

Building, Maintaining, and Strengthening Relationships

Notable in the stories of these boundary spanners was their inherent regard for partners and the relationships that they fostered which were clearly built on constructs of mutuality and respect. Boundary spanners highly valued the contributions of the other partner. Shari worked to validate and encourage her interns, realizing that they were in a period of their professional development rife with challenges and insecurities. Terry recognized the importance of demonstrating care, respect, and commitment to in-service teachers and collaborating with them authentically in their struggles and concerns. Carol heard the concerns of her colleagues at the county level and helped make transparent the commitment of the university to the development of positive academic learning trajectories for students and schools. Dee valued and recognized the needs and pressures faced by all stakeholders in the partnership and worked to be certain that these concerns were ameliorated. These boundary spanners were intentional and reciprocal, demonstrating care and commitment, and literally stood in the gap on behalf of all of those involved in the partnership.

The ability to empathize and to understand the situation and challenges of the other was an extremely salient theme for each of these women and was a critical part of the meaningful relationships that they were able to forge, maintain, and develop. The continuity between these boundary spanners and those that they collaborated with was critical for the bonds of trust and openness to develop and for all individuals to feel safe to express their authentic needs and to work to have those needs and concerns met. This type of continuity and trust-based relating must be present if we are to envision new possibilities for collaborative relationships across university and public school contexts that support the development of all invested (Wiseman & Nason, 1995).

Navigating Across Contexts While Utilizing Prior Experiences and Expertise

Each of our boundary spanners utilized her specifically situated knowledge and skills to increase understanding and collaboration as she navigated across partnering contexts. One important aspect of boundary spanning is the opportunity to return to one's own experience and history in ways that utilize first hand knowledge to inform his or her new position. Clearly, each of the individuals highlighted in this chapter was substantively influenced by that which she valued and saw as relevant and important. Each identified issues and concerns which were salient to her own previous experiences and implemented processes of support which were relevant to the needs she had experienced in her previous roles. These understandings of specific roles, challenges, and contexts critically shaped the actions of these women and the ways that they engaged with colleagues in their new spaces. Because Shari, Terry, Carol, and Dee were able to articulate the authenticity, importance, and relevance of the concerns of individuals on both sides of the partnership, they were quite literally able to speak the discourses, to translate and discuss the tensions, and to problem solve in ways that outsiders to either context were less able to accomplish.

We note, however, that boundary spanners are informed by their own experiences and that there are limits to the transferability of their knowledge. Just as relationships are specific and intentionally created, so too was the knowledge that was grounded in specific school sites and ways of working with faculty and administrators in specific programs. Shari supervised interns in her classroom who had been through the teacher preparation she herself had matriculated from two years earlier. Terry found that her own needs and ways of working as a classroom teacher were foundational to the opportunities she provided for her pre-service and in-service teachers. Carol worked to articulate her own depth of understanding of the research initiatives of the partnership in order to provide insight to her new colleagues. Dee, due to her long and successful career in the metropolitan area, had much to capitalize upon, and her knowledge and skills were most fully utilized as she navigated a range of contexts. Each of our boundary spanners brought specific first-hand experiences and understandings that guided their actions and advocacy for the partnership (and stakeholders) in specific and intentional ways. The extent to which the new role was linked to their specific backgrounds seemed foundational in the boundary spanners' abilities to develop trust and to use their understanding of others' realities (Many, Fisher, Ogletree, & Taylor, 2009), elements which have been discussed as key to informing and improving PDS initiatives (Robinson & Darling-Hammond, 2005; Wiseman & Nasan, 1995).

Shari, Terry, Carol, and Dee have strong ties with the university and are knowledgeable of the resources that may be available to teachers, schools, and systems. They are able to navigate and utilize these resources in a range of ways, including such opportunities as locating professional development, grants, advisory committees, and mentor teachers. In addition, their in-depth knowledge of clinical teacher preparation programs and research projects allows them to make important connections between university and school initiatives, curricula, and improvement plans in order maximize the effectiveness of the partnerships.

The boundary spanners in this study and in previous research (Buxton, et al., 2005; Stevens, 1999) provided valuable and much needed information about how to function in both school and university environments. Over the years of our PDS initiative, the unique culture and rules of engagement between the university and each school district and partner school has become apparent. Boundary spanners help all parties navigate those cultures, thus ensuring a strong and effective working relationship (Collay, 1995, Sandholtz et al., 1990).

Envisioning Change and Reconstructing Partnerships

Our boundary spanners are particularly adept at imagining and bringing in to being new ways of acting and collaborating in our partnership. Due to their lived experiences, they can envision ways in which the professional development school partnerships can bridge educational communities and be mutually beneficial and contributory. Specifically, they can inform PDS participants whose work has been shaped in one context only. By establishing positions for boundary spanners that take into account their specific knowledge, expertise, and experience, we will be best able to form long term collaborations that allow educators to truly stand in the gap between universities and public schools, theory and practice, and ensure that the needs, voices, and concerns of all are heard and accounted for in ways that can guide our school-university partnerships (Buxton, et al., 2005).

Boundary spanners have the potential to blur the lines and work to develop and benefit both the schools and university simultaneously in ways that increase professionalism, learning, and student impact and that have the potential to inform our field. Shari recommends school-based university liaisons who are supportive rather than evaluative and able to negotiate the types of support for pre-service and in-service teachers that could benefit all. Terry works to support pre-service and in-service teachers simultaneously as she engages in clinical teacher preparation and in-service teacher professional development. Carol attempts to articulate and meet the needs of partners on either side of the boundary. Dee encourages university faculty to engage in meaningful and longitudinal ways with school partners and to see their role as one that is accountable to the public school partners as well as to the priorities of the university.

Boundary spanners who blur these borders are particularly critical. It would behoove our partnership to continue to recruit adjunct professors or part-time instructors who continue to work in partner school districts and PK–12 teachers who can co-teach with university faculty in field-based classes and/or mentor student teachers. By supporting the integration of university faculty as long term consultants to schools and systems to provide ongoing professional development or other services, we can continue to blur the boundaries between university and the public schools.

SUMMARY

Our partnerships for teacher development and clinical teacher preparation in the PDS networks, and specifically the individuals who span the boundaries of these partnerships, have taught us many lessons. Partnerships with a range of schools and systems are inherently complex. The needs, cultures, expectations, and contexts of a range of programs, departments, schools, and systems intersect, leaving much room for idiosyncratic and responsive ways of being and working together. This, however, does not come easily. We found that boundary spanners are in a unique position to mediate these collaborations due to their strong relationships, their contextually situated and personal knowledge and skills, their ability to mediate the discourses, and their inherent opportunities to re-imagine ways of collaborating to meet the needs of all partners. Stevens (1999) posited that boundary spanners are positioned well to interpret, communicate, and extend relationships between university and school based partners. We found that these boundary spanners were able to create and extend relationships which validated, supported, and encouraged a range of partners due to their continuity of engagement and to their inherent ability to empathize with the 'not so other' other. They were able to imagine and extend the partnership due to their specific prior knowledge of the contexts. Not only did these individuals help maintain the partnerships (Collay, 1995, Sandholtz et al., 1990), but also they acted as change agents (Buxton et al., 2005) as they negotiated goals and imagined new ways of being through their belief that the partnership must be mutually created, enacted, and supported and that it must benefit and extend the effectiveness and goals of each stakeholder.

Boundary spanners are in a unique position to call into question often unexamined ways in which universities, districts, schools, university and school-based faculty, and teacher candidates interact and to extend traditional relationships of imposition in order to create a more responsive, compassionate, productive, and meaningful collaboration. As delineated by each of the previous boundary spanners who shared their story, their powerful experience has led to a more critical lens from which to view partnerships and professional development schools and to inform our clinical teacher preparation. The insight of boundary spanners is a critical ingredient that is important for relationship building and crucial for any PDS network or clinical teacher education model to thrive. Through attending to the insights of boundary spanners' experience, a much richer partnership has been developed and is more likely to be sustained.

REFERENCES

Aldridge, H., & Herker, D. (1977). Boundary spanning roles and organizational structure. *The Academy of Management Review, 2,* 217–230.

Buxton, C. A., Carlone, H. B., & Carlone, D. (2005). Boundary spanners as bridges of student and school discourses in an urban science and mathematics high school. *School science and mathematics, 105,* 302–312.

Collay, M. (1995). Creating a common ground: The facilitator's role in creating school–university partnerships. In H. G. Petrie (Ed.), *Professionalism, partnership, and power: Building professional development schools* (pp. 145–157). New York: State University of New York Press.

Many, J. E., Fisher, T., Ogletree, S., & Taylor, D. (2009, April). Crisscrossing the university and public school contexts as professional development school boundary spanners. Paper presented at the American Educational Research Association, San Diego, CA.

Robinson, S. & Darling-Hammond, L. (2005).Change for collaboration and collaboration for change: Transforming teaching through school-university partnerships. In L. Darling-Hammond (Ed.), *Professional development schools. Schools for developing a profession* (pp. 203–221). New York: Teachers College Press.

Sandholtz, J., & Finan, E. (1990). Blurring the boundaries to promote school/university partnerships. *Journal of Teacher Education, 49*(1), 13–25.

Stevens, D. D. (1999). The ideal, real, and surreal in school-university partnerships: Reflections of a boundary spanner. *Teaching and Teacher Education, 15,* 287–299.

White, J., & Dozier, D. M. (1992). Public relations and management decision making. In J. E. Grunig (Ed.), *Excellence in public relations and communication management* (pp. 91–108). Hillsdale, NJ: Lawrence Erlbaum.

Wiseman, D. L., & Nason, P. L. (1995). The nature of field-based teacher education experience. *Action in Teacher Education, 17*(3), 1–12.

CHAPTER 4

POSSIBILITIES FOR CLINICAL TEACHER EDUCATION

Four Stories of Field-Based Courses Taught at Professional Development School Sites

Mary Ariail, Caitlin McMunn Dooley, Susan Swars, and Laura Smith
Georgia State University

Clinical teacher education is a powerful way to strengthen teacher preparation by strengthening the bonds between the university and professional development school (PDS) sites. We believe connections between university teacher preparation courses and school settings are essential to improving teacher education. Clift and Brady's (2005) synthesis of the research on methods courses and clinical experiences concluded that pre-service teachers often struggle to translate concepts learned in methods courses into their field placement classrooms. They argue that clinical experiences in PDSs can "decrease the discrepancies between advocated practice and situated practice, thus increasing the congruence of messages between the school and university contexts" (p. 331).

Clinical Teacher Education, pages 55–73
Copyright © 2011 by Information Age Publishing
All rights of reproduction in any form reserved.

In this chapter, we describe four specific ways in which our university and neighboring PK–12 schools have created clinical experiences within a PDS structure via university courses taught on-site at PDS schools. Specifically, we detail variations in how clinical teacher education experiences were developed within the context of a PDS partnership. There is no prescribed agenda for establishing PDS partnerships, so partners are free to design programs that are unique to each school and teacher preparation program. Relationships between university teacher preparation programs and PDSs are created through a complex matrix of factors, including the needs of the PK–12 school and university, interpersonal relationships among leadership team members, each participant's strengths and interests, and resources. While this lack of specificity may be liberating for those familiar with the benefits of school partnerships, those who are in the early stages of partnership may find it to be confusing, frustrating, or even intimidating. In this chapter we seek to reduce the confusion and frustration by offering several cases that can serve as models for clinical teacher preparation.

As faculty members at the university, we were interested in leveraging our PDS partnership to improve clinical teacher education experiences. Research suggests that PDSs can positively affect teacher candidates. For example, Castle, Fox, and Sounder (2006) conducted a mixed methods study that compared PDS-prepared pre-service teachers with those who were non-PDS. The PDS-prepared candidates scored significantly higher on classroom planning, instruction, management, and assessment than non-PDS candidates. Qualitative data revealed these candidates showed greater ownership of their school and classrooms and a more sophisticated ability to apply and integrate important standards in teacher education (i.e., INTASC). The researchers concluded that the PDS-prepared pre-service teachers were more focused on students, reflective on classroom practices, and mindful of assessment as recursive. Another study by Ridley, Hurwitz, Hacket, and Miller (2005) indicated that PDS-prepared teachers scored significantly higher on teaching effectiveness during their first year of teaching than teachers who were campus-prepared. These candidates were more effective in engaging students at the beginning of a lesson and retaining student interest and involvement throughout the lesson. A PDS model for teacher preparation has also been linked with teacher retention and attrition (Latham & Vogt, 2007). Pre-service teachers prepared in field-based courses at a PDS were more likely to enter and persist in the teaching profession compared with those prepared in a campus-based model. Although PDSs are only one of a multitude of ways that schools and universities may partner together, we believe that they can be a highly effective way to accomplish clinical teacher education.

Clinical field experiences involve more than just teaching university students at PDS sites. These schools offer not only space for classes but also allow for authentic teaching experiences with "real" pupils and resources (such as teachers as guest speakers, books and media, and data) that are situated, relevant, and real (Worthy & Patterson, 2001). Professors gain new understandings about the current milieu of PK–12 schooling while also creating important relationships with PK–12 teachers, students, administrators, and community members (Dangel, et al., 2009). Professional development schools benefit, as well: the pupils receive one-on-one, small-group, or specialized attention to their learning; the in-service teachers witness models of research-supported, best practices that can be enhanced through on-going conversations with professors and students; and administrative teams are provided with support for their schools, their teachers, and their pupils.

CLINICAL TEACHER PREPARATION IN OUR PROFESSIONAL DEVELOPMENT SCHOOLS

In this chapter, four stories are presented with each author describing her own course that is part of a clinical teacher education program. These clinical field experiences effectively address the four components of our PDS network's mission: (1) the preparation of new teachers, (2) faculty development, (3) inquiry directed at improvement of practice, and (4) enhanced student achievement. The courses cross disciplinary boundaries and span grade levels, demonstrating the variety of ways in which field-based courses might be implemented. Three stories focus on courses that were taught at Highlands Elementary School [pseudonym] by professors in Early Childhood Education: Caitlin, Susan, and Laura. Highlands is a highly diverse, Title I elementary school. The student body at Highlands is 68% Hispanic, 19% African American, 6% Asian/Pacific Islander, 4% multiracial, and 3% white. Ninety-two percent of the students are on free or reduced lunch, and 39% are ESOL. The fourth story focuses on a course taught at Pelham Middle School [pseudonym] by Mary, a professor in Middle-Secondary Education. The student body at Pelham is 46% white, 23% African American, 20% Hispanic, 7% Asian/Pacific Islander, and 4% multiracial. Twelve percent are ESOL and 35% are considered economically disadvantaged. The following sections demonstrate various implementations of clinical teacher education.

Teaching Language Arts in an Elementary School: Caitlin's Story

I (Caitlin) teach a language arts methods course for undergraduate students who intend to become elementary teachers. In my course, we focus on reading and writing instruction in the early elementary grades. As one of three literacy-related courses, this six-hour course gives me the opportunity to include daily lessons with children as part of the regular class meeting time. Research on preparing teachers to teach reading and writing indicates that practicum experiences are necessary and important (International Reading Association, 2003; Darling-Hammond & Bransford, 2005). Additionally, preparing teachers to teach diverse populations in urban districts, with students who might need extra care and help in learning to read and write, requires that teacher preparation programs promote articulation among course content, state standards, and contextual factors (Hollins & Guzman, 2006; Snow, Griffin, & Burns, 2005). Clinical experiences within PDSs can provide this articulation; however, not all experiences provide the same opportunities. Literacy teacher educators and researchers have found that closely supervised clinical experiences followed by structured, high-quality field experiences provide the best means for articulation of literacy course content to classroom practice (Anders, Hoffman, & Duffy, 2000). The course reported here is a practicum that aims to connect course content and real-world instruction. It takes place on a PDS campus and involves pre-service teachers teaching reading and writing with elementary students. One pre-service teacher suggested that the clinical experience was a better representation of the rigor of classroom teaching; she said, "When I'm in a non-field-based course, I get all naïve and think teaching will be a cinch. Field based courses are reality and that's what we need!" Another pre-service teacher told me, "I think that it makes you better prepared and feel more comfortable in a classroom. It helps you see how these strategies are implemented in a classroom."

Getting the Kids (and Their Teachers). My course takes place during the school day, so I usually "borrow" a couple of classes for about an hour for each class meeting. To recruit classroom teachers, I present at early morning staff meetings, ask teacher-friends, and respond to administrative requests. No matter how I get classroom teachers on board, I always emphasize how what I am offering will benefit their young pupils as much as my university students. The young children who have been part of my course come away with an extended small group instructional experience that is responsive to their needs and focused on extending their individual learning. I have been approached by family members, teachers, and administrators who ask to have my university students teach in their children's classes. I also have been told by in-service teachers that having the university students in their classroom refreshes their understanding of new ways for literacy instruction, their students, and curricula.

I involve the classroom teachers in planning and conducting the clinical experiences. Prior to the beginning of each semester, we get to know each other and share our expectations. As the university students teach, the teachers stay in the classroom, give feedback, and ask questions just as I do. I check in with the teachers periodically to ask questions such as, "What has surprised you? What are you wondering? What are you learning? What can we do better?" to ensure that we communicate throughout the semester. These questions help me understand how I might better support the in-service teacher.

A Semester At-A-Glance. The university semester is usually 15 weeks long; therefore, my class has 15 meeting days.

The course always starts with one to three days of meetings with only the university students and me. On these days I introduce the syllabus, set expectations for how the semester will unfold, start students on any long-term projects or assignments, and explain each element of the lesson planning guide that they will use for their work with children. I ensure that these days are held at the school so the students become familiar with the surroundings and comfortable with driving off campus. If this is the first time that students have come to this school, I also incorporate a school tour to show them where and how to obtain food and drink, where the restrooms are located, where to get copies made (if possible), and how to check out books and media from the library. While these details might seem mundane, they help students become familiar with the resources that the school has to offer so that they can use these as they teach.

Days four through 14 are the days in which the university students work with children for 45 to 60 minutes out of each class meeting time. These days include a heavy amount of readings, group work, and activities. I usually spend about an hour facilitating a discussion of the readings, an hour facilitating an activity related to the readings, and an hour helping the students to understand some element of their lessons that they are expected to conduct. They spend about an hour teaching (including the transition times to walk to the young children's classrooms and walk back to our classroom). They need about 30 minutes prior to their lessons to plan. And they need about 30 minutes after their lessons to debrief. One pre-service teacher wrote in an evaluation, "I think it's so much better to get hands-on experience. We learn what we need to do, we do it, then we come back and debrief and discuss (so helpful) ☺" This two-hour practicum experience leaves an hour of "discretionary" time that usually gets absorbed into the other elements, used for breaks, or used for class meetings and other management issues.

Day 15 always involves a culminating experience which can take many shapes. For example, we have helped second-graders to write their own books that they presented at an "Author Celebration," and we have helped fourth-graders develop readers' theater productions. The final day of the semester always involves a celebration of our learning with the young children. No matter what the culminating experience might be, it is introduced early in our work with the children so there is a shared goal and purpose for our work together. We send letters home to families at the beginning of the semester explaining our work and asking them to "save the date." About a week prior to the culminating experience, we send another letter home reminding families that they are invited. And on the day of the culminating experience, we prepare the refreshments, ensure that every child has something to share, and enjoy a moment to show appreciation for our shared involvement with young children.

The Structure for Working with Children. Because of the nature of this chapter, I will not provide details about the content-related elements of my course (e.g., readings/discussions, activities, and content). Rather, I will describe how the students carry out lessons with children.

Triads. The university students work in triads. Three university students are assigned to five children. I have found that the triads help students support each other's learning while also providing them with the experience of leading a small group—something they will be expected to do in their regular classrooms once they become teachers. Within their triads, students rotate daily through three roles: (1) planner, (2) teacher, and (3) observer. The planner plans the lessons and ensures that all of the materials are available prior to the lesson. The teacher carries out the lesson of the day. The observer takes anecdotal notes and is, in essence, the "kid-watcher." The person playing a particular role is the one who will be the leader or guide for that part; however, these are shared responsibilities. In other words, the planner works in conjunction with the group as the main facilitator of the group discussion during planning time. The planner is also the one who takes notes and writes the lesson plans in a way that everyone can understand. Likewise, the observer is responsible for taking notes during the lesson and facilitating the debriefing period; however, everyone is expected to be involved in that process.

Lesson plans. The triads are offered an established lesson plan format with particular elements. Because I teach literacy, the format includes literacy-related elements such as a read-aloud, a mini-lesson, working with words, independent writing time, and a sharing time. Each day, the triads fill out these sections of a planning guide that I provide. I explain each part of the lesson format, offering demonstration lessons early in the semester. Later in the semester, I incorporate time for triads to share their own model lessons. This cross-fertilization invigorates the triads to try new ideas. Each daily lesson follows a general format provided by the lesson plan until the final three days. At that point, we focus more readily on a culminating experience.

Taking Advantage of Other Resources. Some other elements of teaching in professional development schools are important to consider.

Guest Speakers. Aside from visiting model classrooms, I ask administrators, staff members, specialists, and community members to come as guest speakers. Being on-site at a PDS creates the comfortable relationship and convenient proximity necessary to maximize this resource. Additionally, guest speakers are provided with a moment of reflection and celebration of their own professional knowledge. Many guests have been thankful for the chance to speak.

Model Classroom Visits. The university students visit model classrooms in the PDS. We enter the classroom and line the walls. I prepare the students with a guide, including a list of questions or "look fors" to guide their attention as they observe in the model classroom. After about 20 minutes of silent observation during which they take notes relating to the guide, the students move in to talk one-on-one with pupils in the classroom. They ask questions like "Tell me about what you're learning" and "What helps your learning?" Whenever possible, the classroom teacher visits us later (perhaps during a planning period) to debrief on her lesson. She tells about what she was trying to do, what went right, what did not, what decisions she made during our observation. The university students ask questions about what they saw and connect it to our readings, mini-lectures, and activities.

School-Based Resources. Many of my students pulled from their own pockets to supply their young pupils with the tools they needed to complete their lessons or travel back to the university campus to find (or create) materials even though the PDS school had resources. I taught them about how to locate and utilize resources that are readily available at the school. This included everything from specialized knowledge (e.g., resource teachers and specialists) to making copies to finding texts. (Of course, within the PDS, I have negotiated this kind of access prior to inviting my students to enjoy these resources.) I helped students navigate the school's resources by introducing school personnel who can help, telling students about the protocol for accomplishing tasks like checking out books or scheduling time in the computer lab, and even asking the media specialist to assign temporary identification numbers to the students so that they can check out materials on their own. This way, the university students did not have to travel back to campus, and they learned how to navigate the school protocols. Sometimes even the in-service teachers learned about untapped resources and how to integrate them into instruction. Most importantly, the children gained access to materials and information beyond what the university students could afford on their own.

Connecting to the Community through a Family Math Night: Laura's Story

I (Laura) teach a mathematics methods course for undergraduate students who plan to become elementary school teachers. I was aware of the excellent resources and relationships already established by our PDS team at Highlands and wanted to take advantage of the opportunity to work with the school to fulfill its needs while supporting my own instruction.

Getting Started. Prior to the school year, the Highland school administrators, director of the Parent Center, University PDS Liaison, and instructors from the university met to examine Highland's school improvement plan and decide on specific action items that would help to accomplish the new goals for the academic year. One main area of focus was the great desire to increase parental involvement and support at the school. The director of the Parent Center presented ideas for parent meetings (a requirement of all Title I schools). As we discussed our individual needs and goals, implementing a co-sponsored Family Math Night seemed like an opportunity to involve the university students, school staff, children, and parents in a collaborative event to support learning in the area of mathematics. A Family Math Night is a fun, interactive event for elementary school children and their parents to engage in math topics and activities beyond everyday class work (Stenmark, Thompson, & Cossey, 1986). During a Math Night, children and parents participate in various modules or stations providing hands-on activities and resources around different mathematical standards. A Math Night provides an opportunity for parents to gain a better understanding of the school's curriculum while also providing resources and ideas to support math learning at home.

With a small staff of two people, the Parent Center at Highlands could not solely sponsor such an endeavor, and teachers had been reluctant to commit involvement in past years. The opportunity to co-sponsor the event would also provide the university students an authentic experience in collaborating with school support resources such as the Parent Center. The Family Math Night was approved, a date set, and the event was included as a scheduled class session in my mathematics methods course.

Presenting the Plan. The university students shaped every aspect of the Family Math Night project. As a class, we outlined three important goals that would be necessary to make this project worthwhile. Our goals were to 1) participate in a unique opportunity to "learn and live" what it takes to sponsor a school-wide event, 2) interact and communicate with parents (most of whom were non-English speaking) outside of the classroom, and 3) learn to teach elementary mathematics concepts through innovative techniques. The collaborative event also addressed the call from the National Council of Teachers of Mathematics (NCTM) for students, teachers, administrators, and parents to become partners in building high-quality mathematics programs for their children (NCTM, 2000).

Planning and Development. The university students were very supportive of the project and eager to begin the planning. The director of the Parent Center joined us during a class session to negotiate the roles and responsibilities for each group. The Parent Center director agreed to secure a location, conduct the advertising and on-site registration, and provide a small budget for consumable materials. The university students were responsible for selecting, designing, and implementing all math activities, creating a resource list, and creating a design for the setup of each math station.

A portion of each class session in the math methods course was devoted to the planning and development of the project. The university students spent this time examining a variety of mathematics teaching resources and curricula, selecting possible activities, and determining materials and supplies. The university students quickly realized a need to streamline the research and narrow the content focus in math. A specific content focus also provided more continuity among the math stations allowing for a richer and deeper learning experience during the Math Night. In order to determine the mathematical standard(s) for focus, we utilized school-based resources such as the school's Assessment Coordinator and the classroom mentor teachers. During one class session, the Assessment Coordinator conducted a seminar on analyzing standardized test data to inform planning and teaching. Assessment data from the previous year at Highlands suggested that a focus in the area of geometry and measurement was needed at all grade levels. The classroom teachers concurred that this was a challenging standard to teach and additional experiences would be beneficial.

Using this information, the university students developed six geometry and measurement modules containing two to four activities per module appropriate for grades kindergarten through fifth (K–5). This structure allowed every child to participate in at least one activity at each module. Two to four university students supervised each module and guided the children to developmentally appropriate activities.

Implementation. The Family Math Night event was very successful on many levels and the event demonstrated the power gained from the school-university partnership. The attendance was over eight times the expected number, with 80% of all K–5 classrooms represented. The Parent Center greeted families and used this face-to-face opportunity to update school records and discuss the support resources available at the school. The parents were given an opportunity to become involved and further understand and support their child's learning in mathematics. The university students gained valuable experience in planning and implementing a large-scale instructional project, collaborating with school support personnel, as well as interacting with families and the community. The following quotes from two of the university students support the success of this experience:

> *Student 1*: I enjoyed working with these students and their parents. It was exciting to share a fun and learning educational experience in mathematics with the students, parents, and guests. It is not every day that you get to be in the

presence of students and parents to create a fun and educational learning experience in a particular environment. The excitement of it all was wonderful and overwhelming. I would love to participate in another event such as this one.

Student 2: I loved the interaction with excited children and parents. Although it wasn't planned, my partner and I silently agreed about halfway through the evening to tag team between parents and children. While she helped and talked to the kids, I spoke with parents about everything from who we are and why we're at Highlands, to strategies for teaching or reinforcing math at home. After a while, we switched roles. This provided us with equal opportunities to experience interaction with our different guests.

Overall, the university students' reactions to the Family Math Night project were very positive. They appreciated the opportunity to be involved in an authentic collaborative endeavor to enhance their own teaching and learning.

Components of Success. The PDS partnership and specifically the on-site design of the university courses provided several components that increased the success of this large-scale project. These components are described below.

Collaboration with the school community. During field-based internships, our university students are often limited to collaborating with only their mentor teacher or possibly a few teachers within the assigned grade level. Designing and implementing a school-wide instructional project such as the Math Night allowed the university students an opportunity to collaborate with several different school-based support services. This collaborative experience provided a real-life model for connecting and working in a school community as opposed to teaching in an isolated classroom. In regard to valuing this collaboration, a university student shared, "I liked that the school (Parent Center) was so helpful in putting this event on, especially for a school of Highland's size and population. The staff told us the next day that they couldn't have done it without us, but I know that we couldn't have done it without them!"

Developing personal relationships. The university students developed relationships with the children through their weekly classroom-based internships at this school. The university students talked with the children and personally encouraged them to attend the event along with their parents. This one-on-one encouragement was highly motivating and had a positive effect on attendance.

Making a difference. Opportunities to be responsible for school-based events such as a math night or a science fair helped the pre-service teachers to feel that they were an important part of the school community. This connection fostered a sense of concern for and accountability to the children they teach during their pre-service teaching experiences. Through multiple opportunities provided through the PDS partnership, the realization that they are truly "making a difference" was confirmed. Upon reflecting on the Math Night project, one university student shared the following experience:

> Many of the parents were so excited about their students having so much fun partaking in such educational activities. One parent I spoke with did not even know that her child was so good in math. She said that at home the child would take forever to complete any math work. We drew the conclusion that it had to be the way math was presented during Math Night that made the student actually want to do math. I will definitely try and help parents/ families find more fun ways to work with their child in math.

Planning and implementing a school-wide Family Math Night strengthened the school-university-community partnership with Highlands. The many benefits of the event were equally distributed to all partners, and with collaborative efforts, the logistics, cost and labor involved were not overwhelming.

PDS-Based Science Methods Course: Susan's Story

As university liaison to the PDS, I (Susan) spend one day per week at Highland Elementary supporting the collaborative activities of the school and university. My responsibilities were largely in response to the PDS's needs, and the science education of students was of significant concern to the school's administrators and teachers. Therefore, I developed my science methods course to be taught onsite and to work directly with students and teachers at the Highlands. This three-hour undergraduate science methods courses is for pre-service elementary teachers.

Rationale. Data from the 2006–2007 state-mandated science test indicated that 42% of Highland's fourth grade students did not meet the learning standards. Faced with this problem, the teachers perceived science to be a neglected subject, with greater classroom instructional emphases on the high-stakes content areas of mathematics and literacy. Additionally, teachers believed the pronounced focus on high-stakes testing was diverting attention from the accomplishments and celebration of individual students. In order to address these concerns, I held my science methods course at the PDS and integrated work with pupils.

Considering the needs of pre-service teachers related to teaching science, the research literature indicates that clinical experiences in conjunction with science methods courses are important to teacher development. Davis, Petish, and Smithey's (2006) large scale review of research studies published on teacher development in science reported that science methods courses with accompanying clinical experiences contributed to pre-service teachers developing sophisticated understandings of science instruction and acquiring teaching efficacy in science. Moreover, clinical experiences encouraged pre-service teachers to develop an awareness of the importance of anticipating students' ideas in science. From their synthesis, the researchers concluded there is a "crucial importance of placing pre-service teachers in classrooms before their student teaching experiences" (p. 19).

Studies of campus-based science methods courses have revealed that although these courses afforded opportunities to learn to teach science from a reform perspective, many pre-service teachers in subsequent field placements had great difficulty in implementing such an instructional approach (Clift et al., 2005). In considering this finding, pre-service teachers may hold certain beliefs about teaching and learning in science, but they often do not know how to act on these beliefs or how to deal with the difficulties encountered in doing so. Pre-service teachers need support as they attempt to enact beliefs and practices based on theory from science methods courses.

Implementation. The National Science Education Standards (NSES), as well as the state and school district science standards for the PDS, emphasize the importance of authentic scientific inquiry as a component of learning science, which is a natural process of children asking questions, gathering and examining data to answer these questions, and developing explanations (National Research Council, 1996). This perspective requires substantial paradigm shifts about teaching and learning science for many pre-service teachers. Thus, to facilitate this change, a major goal of my course was for pre-service teachers to develop an understanding of and confidence in scientific inquiry; further, pre-service teachers should be able to create inquiry-based learning environments in science.

Participants in the PDS-based science methods course included 23 elementary pre-service teachers and four fourth-grade teachers at Highland, along with their 75 students. With the science methods course meeting on-site at the PDS, the pre-service teachers were afforded the opportunity to work in the fourth-grade teachers' classrooms to facilitate scientific inquiry projects. The fourth-grade teachers volunteered their classrooms in response to an invitation that was extended to all teachers at this grade level. The invitation outlined expectations for the processes and outcomes of the scientific inquiry projects and more importantly highlighted the benefits to children. I spend one day per week at the school; therefore many of the teachers were familiar with me and my role. This rapport allowed the teachers to feel comfortable in volunteering. I hoped this experience would not only be transformative for my pre-service teachers, but also for the fourth-grade teachers as they observed effective teaching of science through inquiry, thus promoting the simultaneous renewal of both groups. I established ongoing communication with the fourth-grade teachers, meeting with them before, during, and after the project implementation. During these meetings, I provided a full explanation of the scientific inquiry projects as well as addressed their questions and concerns. I wanted them to understand that this experience was a negotiable and flexible process and their suggestions and expertise were welcome.

To facilitate the scientific inquiry projects, the pre-service teachers worked in partnerships with small groups of fourth-grade children across four days (four days in two classrooms, then four days in two other classrooms, for a total of eight days for all four classrooms). On day one, the children generated science-related research questions and planned an investigation for answering these questions. The pre-service teachers prompted their questions through scientific demonstrations, informational literature, and discrepant events. On days two and three, the children conducted their investigations and generated conclusions while pre-service teachers facilitated these processes. On day four, the children, in conjunction with the pre-service teachers, created a project board communicating their scientific inquiry projects. This four-day process resulted in a culminating science fair, where the boards were displayed and the children explained their projects to other students at the PDS while the pre-service teachers supervised. At the end of each day, I debriefed with the pre-service teachers by prompting them to reflect on their work with the children, specifically focusing on children's learning and misunderstandings as well as teaching successes and challenges.

Given this format for the projects, my course schedule was modified, which resulted in the course being front-loaded in the academic semester. I allowed one week between day one and day two to provide the pre-service teachers time to procure materials and informational literature to address the children's research questions. Since the research questions were children-generated and thus distinct, the pre-service teachers needed to buy specific materials for the investigations. The pre-service teachers were provided financial assistance from the university in purchasing these materials. Days two, three, and four occurred within one week to allow for a more seamless learning experience for the children during the inquiry projects.

Outcomes. The clinical field experience within this science methods course resulted in the first ever science fair at Highlands. Feedback from elementary students, teachers, and administrators was overwhelmingly positive. Not only was this a valuable learning experience for the pre-service teachers and children, but the in-service teachers found numerous opportunities to observe examples of effective science teaching through inquiry processes as the pre-service teachers worked with their children. This integrated course addressed the needs and concerns of the stakeholders at the PDS (see rationale). Both the fourth-grade teachers and their children gained a deeper understanding of scientific inquiry; further, the accomplishments of individual children were highlighted and celebrated during the science fair.

To evaluate the effectiveness of the course, I conducted research to examine the pre-service teachers' perceptions of affordances and constraints of the course. The PDS-based course afforded experiences working with pupils that (a) provided an in-context view of what reform science instruction might look like in elementary classrooms, (b) caused the pre-service teachers to attend more closely to children's learning, and (c) reified their beliefs in reform-oriented science instruction. Further, the pre-service teachers overwhelmingly advocated for the continued implementation of the PDS-based science methods course, particularly in light of the pervasive lack of instructional emphasis on science in elementary classrooms. The pre-service teachers perceived the constraints of the course to be associated with time-related issues (e.g., front loaded nature), as well as resource availability at the PDS. Subsequent to this study, I modified the PDS-based science methods course by changing the course structure and providing increased resources, thus addressing these constraints.

After-School Writing Workshop at a Middle School: Mary's Story

Soon after I (Mary) became the university coordinator for Pelham Middle School, I attended a session on clinical field experiences led by Caitlin Dooley at a PDS retreat. Although I had never taught a course that integrated clinical experiences before, I immediately recognized the benefits that this format might offer for a course that I was planning to teach the following spring.

General Course Information. "Theory and Pedagogy in the Teaching of Writing," a three-hour graduate course, is required for masters students majoring in secondary English Education, but it is also open to graduate students in other programs as an elective. My nascent relations with the middle school had already led to conversations about the ways we might help middle-school students improve their writing, and the graduate course I was scheduled to teach was focused on the theories and applications for good writing. Moving the course to the middle-school campus and involving middle-school students and teachers seemed like a natural way to accomplish both goals.

Rationale. Process writing teachers and scholars advocate student-centered approaches to supporting writing development. At least as long ago as the 1980s, literacy educators recognized the benefits of a process-oriented approach to writing (Atwell, 1998; Calkins, 1986; Graves, 1983; Hansen, 1983, 1987), as it frees teachers and students from a rigid, product-oriented writing pedagogy (Graves, 1983). Process writing is often coupled with the writing workshop method, a curricular structure that incorporates topic choice, sustained writing time, teacher and peer conferences, author circles, author chairs, and celebrations (Calkins, 1994; Short, Harste, & Burke, 1996). Despite the abundant research on the benefits of teaching writing as a process, teachers who simply read and talk about process writing are often reluctant to implement process writing in their own classrooms. Voicing their fears of rigid curriculum, overbearing administrators, ubiquitous emphasis on test-taking, and uncooperative students, pre-service and novice teachers sometimes argue that process writing approaches may be too idealistic to work in the "real world" of school. Therefore, teachers who have little or no firsthand experience in process writing often fall back on the more familiar, product-oriented approach. The purpose of the middle-school project, therefore, was two-fold: (1) to increase in-service and pre-service teachers' understanding of the theory and research underlying a process writing approach, its many benefits, and firsthand experience in teaching in this way; and (2) to provide a supportive environment for middle-school students to explore their writing abilities in a writing workshop context.

Implementation. The ten-week after-school writing workshop paired 11 graduate students from the university with 22 sixth-grade students at the middle school in a project that took place within the structure of a 15-week master's level graduate course. The graduate students were beginning teachers, student teachers, teachers who had taught in the past but were not currently teaching, and students who had no teaching experience. The requirements for the middle-school students were as follows: Each participant must (1) be recommended by his or her language arts teacher, (2) express a desire to improve his or her writing, and (3) promise to attend all ten writing workshop sessions.

The graduate students read and discussed a variety of professional readings on the teaching of writing and applied the writing theories in practical experiences with middle-school students. Each graduate student served as a writing coach for two sixth-grade students who had volunteered to participate in the program. Classroom teachers from the school were invited to enroll in the course as university graduate students, or to take the course for PLU (professional learning unit) credits through their school system.

A typical writing workshop day began at 4:00 when the middle-school students were dismissed from school. The graduate class was not scheduled to begin until 4:30, so we utilized the thirty-minute gap in ways that were both fun and educational. After students signed in and had a snack, my graduate teaching assistant, Ellen Hurst, led the students in a series of "Writing Enrichment" exercises. Ellen varied the writing enrichment each week with activities such as a "Writing Jeopardy" game, a "Writing Bingo" game, and a "Funeral for Dead Words" ceremony. When the graduate students arrived at 4:30, they visited with their students for a few minutes and set goals for writing for the day. At 4:45, two graduate students would teach a writing mini-lesson collaboratively. The topic for each mini-lesson was chosen by the middle-school students the week before and focused on one specific topic that the students believed would help their writing. The mini-lesson was followed by independent writing time during which everyone in the room wrote silently for 30 to 40 minutes. Then each graduate student (whom we referred to as the "writing coaches") worked with two middle-school students in a small conference to share and discuss their writing. Students were then invited to share excerpts from their writing with the large group. The session with the middle-school students ended with a brief discussion of what they would like to learn more about during the following week's mini-lesson. After the middle-school students departed, the graduate students discussed their coaching experiences as well as the professional readings that were assigned for the day. Thus, they were able to apply immediately their professional learning as they reflected on and discussed the experiences they had with their students.

Our culminating experience was a celebration of the students' writing at a Writing Fair, which was held at the school on the last day of class. We invited all of the middle-school students' parents, language arts teachers, and school administrators to attend the event. Each participant was given a bound copy of the class book containing each of the "published pieces," and we encouraged the students to read their "published pieces" aloud to the appreciative audience.

Results. Responses from both graduate students and the middle-school students were overwhelmingly positive. Among the graduate students, the most affirming results were the changes in their attitudes toward teaching writing. For example, in January, Candace (a student in her first semester of graduate school who had never taught) expressed her reluctance before the workshop began: "I lack confidence in my writing abilities and I know teaching will push me out of my box to embrace something that I consider to be my weakness." A few weeks later, the same student wrote, "I wish I didn't have to wait until next Fall 2009 to start my student teaching. This course has made me so excited to teach that I want to start NOW!" Comments like these are encouraging because they indicate that the teacher will not only learn about the theories associated with teaching writing as a process, but she will be willing to implement the teaching strategies in her own classroom.

The middle-school students also expressed positive attitudes toward the class. An exit evaluation survey suggested that their biggest complaint was that they wished the lessons were longer! When asked if they thought they had become better writers, 14 said "Yes" and two said "Not sure." No students said "No." These results suggest an increase in students' confidence in their own writing abilities as well as more favorable attitudes toward writing.

DISCUSSION

Although the four stories presented in this chapter varied significantly in the way the authors implemented clinical field experiences, each course was deemed as highly successful by the parties involved. We agree on several elements that contributed to our success. First, and foremost, we respect our collaborative relationship with the teachers and administrators at the PDSs. This respect is evident in our course design—we attended to the needs and desires of school personnel as we determined how to integrate our courses. In one case that meant that we conducted an in-class workshop; in another case, we helped organize an evening Math Night with community and parent support. The PDS partnerships offered fertile ground for relationship building; however, we had to nurture those relationships by attending school meetings, taking time to meet with teachers before and after school, and showing genuine interest in what the school needed from our involvement.

Second, successful implementation of the clinical experiences was dependent on working among a supportive faculty and university administration. Our work was celebrated within our own faculty meetings and in special sessions of our PDS conferences. In addition, many of our courses required extra materials, such as display boards for the science fair and refreshments for families at Math Night. Both the university and school administrators gave willingly from their budgets to support our innovations. These celebrations and financial support not only eased our burdens, but also sent a message to course instructors and students that clinical teacher education is valued and appreciated.

Finally, the success of our courses relied on direct work with children. In each course, our university students worked with students and their families at the PDS schools. Overwhelmingly, the university students commented on the usefulness of practicing with "real" kids and families. We have heard comments like "I never thought it would be this hard!" and "I can't imagine learning how to teach in any other way." We believe that field-based courses support pre-service and novice teachers as they learn through authentic interactions with students, school personnel, and families.

Consistent with the research literature, our experiences suggest that quality teacher preparation programs provide students with clinical experiences that are highly integrated with their coursework (Grossman, 2006). This integration allows for immediate connection of educational theory learned in coursework with practices in classrooms. Levine (2006) argued that an important component of high quality programs are professional development schools, which serve as a setting for integrated field experiences for pre-service teachers. Field experiences in PDSs allow for considerable integration of theory learned in university coursework with practices in PK–12 classrooms. Having conducted courses in PDS schools, we agree that this relationship, when nurtured and respectful, can benefit our university students, the PDS schools, and the pupils whom we all strive to serve through high-quality education.

In this chapter, we have described four ways to implement field-based courses in PDS schools. We hope these stories may serve as a catalyst or a model for those who are considering new or additional ways to promote effective clinical teacher preparation.

REFERENCES

Anders, P.L., Hoffman, J.V., & Duffy, G.G. (2000) Teaching teachers to teach reading: Paradigm shifts, persistent problems, and challenges. In M. Kamil, P. Mosenthal, P. D. Pearson, & R. Barr (Eds.), *The handbook of reading research, Vol. III* (pp. 719–742). Mahwah, NJ: Erlbaum.

Atwell, N. (1998). *In the middle: New understandings about writing, reading, and learning*. Portsmouth, NH: Heinemann.

Calkins, L.M. (1986). *The art of teaching writing*. Portsmouth, NH: Heinemann.

Calkins, L.M. (1994). *The art of teaching writing* (2nd ed.). Portsmouth, NH: Heinemann.

Castle, S., Fox, R. K., & Souder, K. O. (2006). Do professional development schools (PDSs) make a difference? A comparative study of PDS and non-PDS teacher candidates. *Journal of Teacher Education, 57*, 65–80.

Clift, R. T., & Brady, P. (2005). Research on methods courses and field experiences. In M. Cochran-Smith & K. M. Zeichner (Eds.), *Studying teacher education: The report of the AERA Panel on Research and Teacher Education* (pp. 309–424). Mahwah, NJ: Lawrence Erlbaum.

Dangel, J., Dooley, C. M., Swars, S., Truscott, D., Smith, S., & Williams, B. (2009). Professional development schools: A study of change from the university perspective. *Action in Teacher Education, 30*, 4, 3–17.

Darling-Hammond, L., & Bransford, J. (Eds.). (2005). *Preparing teachers for a changing world: What teachers should learn and be able to do*. Washington, D.C.: Jossey-Bass.

Davis, E. A., Petish, D., & Smithey, J. (2006). Challenges new science teachers face. *Review of Educational Research, 76*, 607–652.

Graves, D. H. (1983). *Writing: Teachers and children at work*. Portsmouth, NH: Heinemann.

Grossman, P. (2006). Research on pedagogical approaches in teacher education. In M. Cochran-Smith & K. M Zeichner (Eds.), *Studying teacher education: The report of the AERA Panel on Research and Teacher Education* (pp. 425–476). Mahwah, NJ: Lawrence Erlbaum.

Hansen, J. (1983) The author's chair. *Language Arts, 60*, 176–183.

Hansen, J. (1987). *When writers read*. Portsmouth, NH: Heinemann.

Hollins, E., & Guzman, M. T. (2006). Research on preparing teachers for diverse populations. In M. Cochran-Smith & K. M Zeichner (Eds.), *Studying teach-

er education: The report of the AERA Panel on Research and Teacher Education (pp. 477–548). Mahwah, NJ: Lawrence Erlbaum.

International Reading Association (2003). *Prepared to make a difference: Research evidence on how some of America's best university programs prepare teachers of reading.* Newark, DE: Author.

Latham, N. I., & Vogt, W.P. (2007). Do professional development schools reduce teacher attrition: Evidence from a longitudinal stuffy of 1,000 graduates. *Journal of Teacher Education, 58,* 153–167.

Levine, A. (2006, September). *Educating school teachers.* Retrieved on May 11, 2009, from http://www.edschools.org/teacher_report.htm

National Council of Teachers of Mathematics. (2000). Principles and standards for school mathematics. Reston, VA: NCTM.

National Research Council. (1996). *National science education standards.* Washington, DC: National Academy Press.

Ridley, D. S., Hurwitz, S., Hacket, M. R. D., & Miller, K. K. (2005). Comparing PDS and campus-based preservice teacher preparation: Is PDS-based preparation really better? *Journal of Teacher Education, 56,* 46–56.

Short, K.G., Harste, J.C. with Burke, C. (1996) *Creating classrooms for authors and inquirers* (2nd Ed.). Portsmouth, NH: Heinemann.

Snow, C. E., Griffin, P, & Burns, S. M. (Eds.). (2005). *Knowledge to support the teaching of reading.* NY: Jossey-Bass.

Stenmark, J., Thompson, V. & Cossey, R. (1986). *Family math.* Berkeley, CA: Lawrence Hall of Science.

Worthy, J. & Patterson, J. (2001). "I can't wait to see Carlos!": Pre-service teachers, situated learning, and personal relationships with students. *Journal of Literacy Research, 33,* 303–344.

CHAPTER 5

EXAMINING PDS PARTNERSHIPS WITH SURVEY ITEMS

Assessing Perception of Fidelity of Implementation Using the NCATE PDS Standards

William L. Curlette and Susan Ogletree
Georgia State University

As noted in the chapters throughout this book, our approach to clinical teacher education with the sites in our urban network was guided by the NCATE professional development school standards (NCATE, 2001). As we considered how to know if our university/public school collaboration was effective, we realized it would be important to understand the extent to which teachers working within our school sites perceived the PDS standards as being present in our implementation. To help accomplish this goal, we created a fidelity survey with close-ended items to assess the degree of implementation of each standard as part of our evaluation of our PDS network. We administered our survey each year for four years, thus providing a longitudinal view of the implementation of PDS standards across the evolution of our partnership.

Clinical Teacher Education, pages 75–91
Copyright © 2011 by Information Age Publishing
75

In this chapter, we will provide the reader with an overview of how clinical teacher education programs can develop fidelity instruments and then use such an instrument in research to understand and improve their partnership. We begin by discussing the NCATE standards and our initial development of the fidelity survey. The survey includes items related to the standards, phrased in a way to allow us to understand teachers' *perceptions of the presence* of those PDS standards in their own school. Next, we draw on our own data to demonstrate the extent to which teachers in our PDS schools endorsed items that reflected the presence of a standard and how we used this as a measure of fidelity of implementation of our PDS program. We were in a unique position to conduct this research because we had PDSs and matched comparison schools participating in our project. Consequently, we could compare the percentage of endorsement of an item in PDSs to comparable schools which were not professional development schools. As far as can be determined from our literature review, this approach to viewing PDS implementation has not been previously conducted. Although the nature of the survey creation and our analysis of the findings does get technical in the sections which follow, we feel the inclusion of such quantitative analyses makes an important contribution along with the other qualitative findings shared in other chapters in this text. Following our presentation of the results from our fidelity study, we conclude our chapter with a discussion of what we have learned and our thoughts for future directions.

THE NCATE PDS STANDARDS

The development of the NCATE (2001) PDS standards brought validation to the work of professional development schools. Prior to the development of NCATE standards, many efforts had been made to document the effectiveness of PDSs. Early studies primarily addressed the theory, implementation, and description of PDSs. Researchers also documented and explored the nature and impact of district-school-university partnerships (Abdal-Haqq, 1988; Book, 1996; Campy, 2000). By establishing the standards, NCATE sought to increase the awareness of the movement, to establish an open and exploratory culture, to increase planning and evaluation, to focus on professional development and educational renewal, and to integrate the work of the PDS with other schools in the district and with university programs. The ultimate goal of the PDS movement was to improve students' academic achievement while decreasing the academic achievement gap that persists between ethnic and cultural groups within the United States.

From the beginning, the NCATE PDS standards were touted as a model that provided top-down support for bottom-up reform (Darling-Hammond & McLaughlin, 1995) through the use of practitioner wisdom and experience. The data used to construct the standards were captured through an in-depth survey (Tractman, 1998), and researchers, policymakers, teachers, and leaders of the PDS movement convened in Chicago for a national conference on professional development schools to collaborate in creating the standards (Freeman, 1998; Levin & Churins, 1999).

An Overview of the Five Standards

The NCATE PDS standards consist of five separate standards; however, because the standards are to be viewed holistically (NCATE, 2001), the five standards can often overlap in scope. The five standards are (a) learning community, (b) accountability and quality assurance, (c) collaboration, (d) equity and diversity, and (e) structures, resources, and roles. These standards are constructed for use as the framework for assessment of individual PDS communities in relation to the degree to which PDS initiatives are aligned to the NCATE rubric. Often, through a review/renewal process, PDS partnerships are made aware of the strengths and weaknesses within the collaboration. Such an awareness can often lead to significant improvement in the PDS partnership.

Learning community. The first standard, learning community, is often seen as one of the most important to the development of a beginning PDS partnership. The development of PK–12 students, teacher interns, and PDS partners cannot be accomplished without the overarching support of a committed learning community. The strength of inquiry-based practice is seen through the results obtained from the improvement of teaching pedagogy, student academic achievement, and change in policies and procedures of the partnering institutions.

Accountability and quality assurance. The second standard, accountability and quality assurance, focuses on identifying and upholding professional teaching and learning standards within the PDS partnership and before the public at large. Clearly articulated criteria for participation in the PDS movement should be apparent at both the individual school and institutional levels. Agreed upon assessment strategies are collaboratively developed and implemented. Interns, schools, university faculty, and the community analyze and share data collected through the PDS implementation that pertains to student learning outcomes and other potential outcomes of the process. Perhaps most importantly, the collected data are used continuously to improve student academic achievement, intern training, and teaching pedagogy.

Collaboration. The third standard, collaboration, encourages PDS partners to build authentic, mutually beneficial, interdependent relationships. These relationships become the keystones for continuous and future development of the PDS. Cross-institutional relationships—specifically between school and university participants—benefit the PDS as a whole. Cross-institutional relationships provide a space for the dialogue necessary for university and public school participants to create meaningful linkages among theory, research, and instructional practices. Cross-institutional relationships can lead to a synergistic improvement of teaching and learning pedagogy across PK–12 students, interns, school teachers and university faculty.

Diversity and equity. Diversity and equity in learning comprise the fourth NCATE standard, which focuses primarily on the policies and procedures related to these two areas. Participants in any PDS implementation must take as their mission the commitment to ensure equitable learning opportunities for everyone involved in the PDS community. This commitment requires continuous diligent review of programs offered throughout the PDS partnership. Efforts to establish and maintain equity in schools and universities focus on the responsibility all PDS participants have to provide a quality education for every student, intern, teacher, and university faculty member. Doing so requires a focus on training highly qualified, results-oriented teachers, so that each PDS classroom can be staffed with a highly qualified teacher. Another equity issue is the balanced distribution of resources, such as textbooks and supplies, so that every student's educational needs are met.

Structures, resources, and roles. The fifth and final PDS standard focuses on structures, resources, and roles. This standard provides the framework for the establishment of governance procedures necessary for support of the PDS partnership's mission. An emphasis of this standard is the continuous systematic review of the roles and responsibilities of the PDS partnership members. Through the established governance framework, collaborative modifications of the roles and responsibilities can be on-going in an effort to meet the frequently changing needs of the PDS partner participants. Resource acquisition is important and necessary for sustaining the efforts of the PDS. All partners are expected to broker resources from a variety of sources to support established PDS work and allow for expansion of innovative pedagogy. While a successful PDS school can exist on minimal resources, additional resources are often required to put into effect the recommendations by the community, parents, teachers, and university faculty. Resource acquisition is directly related to the communications among and between all partners, including the public, policy makers, and professional audiences of the work being conducted (NCATE, 2001).

Holistic Nature of the Standards

As we have mentioned, the five articulated NCATE PDS standards are not exclusive entities. NCATE recommends that these standards should be viewed holistically as they often overlap. Additionally, because professional development schools and the PDS partnership are constantly changing in response to changes in administration, teaching staff, student population, political activities, and community requests, PDSs may demonstrate both improvement and regression across time. The NCATE PDS standards provide a guide for PDS partnerships to help them identify how well they are adhering to the guidelines and to advise them as they attempt to negotiate their continuation as a professional development school within their own social, political, and academic circumstances. This is knowledge meant not just for the leaders of the partnership but rather for all participants, including teaching interns, school teachers, and their students. An effective professional development school partnership values the need for comprehensive communication among all of its participants.

Assessing Fidelity of Implementation

In order to understand our efforts to design a fidelity study focusing on the degree to which our PDS sites were reflective of the NCATE PDS standards, we now turn to a discussion of considerations which must be taken into to account when designing such inquiry and interpreting the results. The degree to which a program is implemented as intended by developers is known as the fidelity of implementation (Dusenbury, Brannigan, Falco & Lake, 2004). The likelihood that a multiyear project will be implemented exactly as planned is low. Implementation of innovative social programs does not occur in isolation, and the programs are not self-executing (Petersilia, 1990). In the case of a PDS implementation, pervasive commitment and communication keep participants at all levels involved and invested in the program, and we assert that the greater this involvement, the more closely the program will maintain fidelity during implementation. Moreover, PDS structures help to break down isolation and encourage collaboration in an effort to empower teachers to think through standards of practice (Darling-Hammond et al., 1995). This task can be accomplished as the key actors begin to explore PDS standards and correlate them to the implementation of the PDS program.

In 1987, Bickman identified the importance of documenting the implementation of a given program for a specific model. Because PDS models tend to be context-specific, the NCATE PDS standards provide a universal framework for collaborative discussion and model implementation. This framework can provide guidance to PDS partnerships when internal or external influences complicate the model as they are implementing it. The standards help PDS partnerships avoid the lack of specificity or classification for program implementation that can cause models to stray or drift out of alignment from the intended model (Bond, 1991). As part of the design team for our professional development school partnership, we knew it was important that the implementation be considered with the understanding that school teachers would use what they learned through program participation in unique ways within their classrooms.

Assessing fidelity of implementation has been relatively neglected in program outcome research (Durlak, 1998). Gresham (1989) stated that most educational researchers assume the program implementation will follow the prescribed protocol. A possible reason for this neglect is that assessing implementation fidelity comprehensively does not easily lend itself to quantitative analysis. However, an initial and less comprehensive quantitative assessment can provide a first step toward an understanding of program implementation. Then other sources of information can be employed to help understand the complex, multidimensional continuum that consists of characteristics such as teachers' attitudes and behaviors and broader variables, such as frequency of collaboration, consistent mutual support, and accurate conveyance of information. Educators generally agree that there will always be some degree of variation in context causing a difference in program implementation (Elias, 1997; Meyer, Miller & Herman, 1993), and the professional development school partnership should be designed to accommodate that variance. Thus, we do not see assessing fidelity of implementation as a method to get the program *back on track* but rather as a way of monitoring what variances have occurred so that we can consider the causes of those variances as we plan for future years of the program. Quantitative indicators from a fidelity survey can reveal some of these variances and stimulate a deeper discussion of program implementation.

Allowing for variance does complicate assessment of fidelity of implementation. Gresham, MacMillan, Beebe-Frankenberger, and Bocian (2000) argued that to identify the degree of implementation in and between schools, an evaluator should be able to state that the program is implemented as planned and not changed substantially by those responsible for the implementation of the program. However, in the case of a PDS implementation, evaluators and program leaders must recognize that they are involved in the academic development of actual students, and their interests are the most important consideration at times during program implementations. Continuing a program component, when changing it would improve the learning environment for students, violates the trust these young people have put in their teachers, their schools, and all participants in the PDS partnership. Assessing the PDS model remains an important consideration throughout the PDS implementation, but, for us, it is never the most important consideration.

As the NCATE PDS standards were written from an administrative perspective (although all levels of participants were included in the development process), we decided to explore the question of the perceived degree of implementation of the project by classroom teachers as it relates to the standards. Thus, we designed the PDS Differential Implementation Fidelity Inventory (PDS DIF-I) based on the NCATE standards to give us an idea of how well the NCATE standards captured the developmental operationalization of the perceptions of the participating teachers. The PDS DIF-I version 1 is the formal name of the instrument we developed as a fidelity survey.

Survey Development and Administration

For the purposes of measuring the presence of activities, beliefs, or values representative of the NCATE PDS standards or specific aspects of these unique to our PDS, we ultimately selected 67 items across the five scales. The items were written to be responded to on the following scale: *Yes, No,* or *Unsure. Unsure* was included as an option because some of the items asked teachers to give their perceptions of activities in their school or beliefs and values held by others, and they legitimately may have been unsure. A *Yes* response indicated that the teacher endorsed the item; thus, each item measured the presence of the activity but not its intensity.

The survey was administered on the Internet and was made available to teachers both in the twelve PDSs and in their matched Comparison Schools (CSs). The CSs were matched on race/ethnic group, previous academic achievement, and percentage of students eligible for free or reduced meals. In year one, all schools in the study had at least 50% of the students eligible for free or reduced meals.

We wanted teachers' perceptions of PDS implementation across a whole academic year. Therefore, we administered the survey the following fall, asking PDS or CS teachers about their experiences concerning the previous year. An additional reason for administering the survey with respondents looking back in fall at the previous year was that the school systems did not want data collection in spring near the close of a school year because of student achievement testing and other school activities. We offered a $10 gift card as a token of appreciation to each teacher who completed the survey. Our sample included a total of 658 teachers from four administrations of the survey. The numbers of respondents in PDS and CS schools for each year can be found in Table 5.1. (These sample sizes can be used in conjunction with tables of results later in this chapter to aid in the interpretation of statistical significance and effect sizes.)

To check the representativeness of the sample of teachers using demographics, we selected year three and compared sample estimates for gender and race/ethnic groups from questions on the fidelity survey to population values from our state for the schools involved in this study. For gender, the sample estimates from the survey were 21.7% males and 78.2% females, in comparison to the state population data of 27.8% males and 72.2% females. For each race/ethnic group, the following list gives the sample percentage estimates first and the population percentage values second: African-

TABLE 5.1 Sample Sizes for PDS and Comparison School Groups

Year	N (PDS Teachers)	N (Comparison School Teachers)
1	93	38
2	129	77
3	76	128
4	70	47

American 47.9% compared to 54.2%; Caucasian 42.5% compared to 40.4%; Hispanic 3.2% compared to 2.7%; Asian 2.7% compared to 2.0%; other with Native American combined 3.6% compared to 1.0%. This data provides some evidence for the representativeness of the sample; a quota sampling approach may eventually be employed to force the same percentages in each group, but this method would result in a loss of sample size.

Our plan for data analysis was to work primarily at the item level and test essentially the difference in percentages of *Yes* and *Not Yes* responses for the PDSs versus the CSs for each item. The *Not Yes* responses included both the *No* and *Unsure* data. To summarize some of the results, we employed a vote counting procedure by counting statistically significant results. Nevertheless, we recognized that effect sizes are also important, so for most of the tables of results which we discuss, the actual percentages are reported.

UNDERSTANDING THE RESULTS OF OUR FIDELITY SURVEY

To conduct the primary data analysis, we constructed two by two tables for each of the items where one dimension of a table was either a *Yes* or *Not Yes* response and the other dimension was PDS or CS. To analyze these two by two contingency tables, we employed Fisher's two tailed exact test with alpha equal to .05. To improve the statistical conclusion validity by conducting an alternative analysis (Shadish, Cook, & Campbell, 2002) for the NCATE PDS indicators, we created scales based on content analysis of items, ran coefficient alpha reliabilities and then a multivariate analysis of variance to test vectors of means.

One way we viewed the results was to count the number of statistically significant results from the contingency table analysis, which essentially tested the differences in percentages between the PDS teacher responses and the CS teacher responses. Of the 268 comparisons (i.e., 67 items times four years with PDS v. CS), 120 or 45% were statistically significant in favor of PDS. These results indicate that the NCATE PDS standards were perceived as being more present in PDSs than in CSs and provide evidence at the construct level for the fidelity of implementation. Only one of the 268 comparisons was statistically significant in favor of CSs (item six in year three, which is discussed later).

We disaggregated this vote count of 120 significant results by the NCATE PDS standards in order to show which standards had the most statistically significant comparisons between the PDS and CS teachers. To obtain the number of possible comparisons between PDS and CS teachers, the number of items on each standard is multiplied by four years to obtain the number of actual comparisons for each standard. Next, the number of statistically significant results is divided by the number of actual comparisons and multiplied by 100 to obtain the percentage of items from each standard more endorsed as present in the PDS schools. These calculations are shown in Table 5.2. As seen in Table 5.2, the standard with the most items which had statistically significant percentage differences between the PDS and CS teachers was "collaboration," which was followed by the "structures, resources, and roles" standard. The standard for "learning community" showed the least number of items which had statistically significant differences in percentages of *Yes* responses between PDS and CS teachers. This finding assumes that the items written for a standard were representative of that standard, which we believed to be the case based on our item assignments. Furthermore, we did note that the PDS NCATE standards themselves overlap each other, making item assignment less certain in some instances.

Another way we viewed the results in order to see the impact of the PDS was to compile the items which had statistically significant results each year across all four years. These 16 items are shown in Table 5.3. Although the

TABLE 5.2   Percentage of Statistically Significant Items Favoring PDS for each of the Five NCATE PDS Standards

NCATE PDS Standard	No. of Items	No. of Items times 4 Years (i.e., No. of 2 × 2 Tables)	No. of Statistically Significant Results	Percentage of Statistically Significant Results	Rank Order
1: Learning Community	17	68	16	23.5	5
2: Accountability and Quality Assurance	15	60	19	31.7	4
3: Collaboration	11	44	39	88.6	1
4: Diversity and Equity	18	72	28	38.9	3
5: Structures, Resources, and Roles	6	24	18	75.0	2

Note: All statistically significant results summarized in Table 5.2 had a higher percentage of *Yes* responses in favor of PDS schools.

TABLE 5.3 Gains in Percentages of Yes Responses for Teachers from Comparison and PDS Schools for Items Which Were Statistically Significant all Four Years

Item No./Stand.	Item	Year 1	Year 2	Year 3	Year 4
	During the last year . . .	$D = PDS_Y\% - CS_Y\%$ $[PDS_U\%, CS_U\%]$			
14/S1	I was aware that my school was in a collaborative partnership with a university.	59 = 93 − 34 [2, 8]	54 = 92 − 38 [2, 9]	57 = 91 − 34 [3, 15]	29 = 91 − 62 [4, 9]
15/S1	my school and a university worked together in an effort to see that best practice activities were integrated into overall school improvement priorities.	38 = 70 − 32 [19, 45]	51 = 77 − 26 [18, 39]	29 = 56 − 27 [28, 47]	37 = 69 − 32 [27, 47]
16/S1	I participated in the collaborative partnership between my school and a university.	39 = 60 − 21 [2, 5]	41 = 62 − 21 [5, 13]	30 = 51 − 21 [12, 13]	31 = 46 − 15 [13, 15]
24/S1	I had responsibilities within the university partnership.	22 = 38 − 16 [7, 16]	25 = 38 − 13 [3, 7]	18 = 27 − 9 [7, 11]	17 = 21 − 4 [11, 9]
33/S3	the collaboration between university personnel and school personnel expanded to include others from the community.	18 = 31 − 13 [53, 71]	15 = 29 − 14 [64, 55]	17 = 27 − 10 [59, 75]	15 = 21 − 6 [71, 79]
36/S3	the university collaboratively coordinated the placement of teacher candidates in my school.	25 = 41 − 16 [46, 66]	30 = 47 − 17 [43, 48]	34 = 47 − 13 [45, 69]	28 = 39 − 11 [56, 68]
37/S3	my school and the university had a whole-school commitment to the professional development-partnership.	31 = 47 − 16 [38, 66]	39 = 53 − 14 [38,51]	34 = 48 − 14 [40, 69]	37 = 54 − 17 [39, 66]

Item	Statement				
38/S3	my school and the university collaboratively planned professional development that targeted student learning focus.	30 = 48 – 18 [40, 66]	32 = 52 – 20 [39, 48]	30 = 45 – 15 [43, 70]	30 = 47 – 17 [46, 64]
39/S3	the university faculty worked with teachers in my school who mentored teacher candidates.	42 = 55 – 13 [33, 71]	39 = 52 – 13 [42, 58]	30 = 43 – 13 [41, 70]	39 = 50 – 11 [43, 72]
40/S3	the university faculty assisted mentor teachers in developing coaching skills as needed.	34 = 45 – 11 [40, 71]	27 = 39 – 12 [52,57]	22 = 33 – 11 [53, 72]	26 = 37 – 11 [54, 70]
41/S3	the university faculty worked collaboratively with teachers in my school to plan research.	17 = 28 – 11 [54, 74]	16 = 29 – 13 [63, 56]	18 = 27 – 9 [59, 77]	18 = 24 – 6 [69, 77]
62/S3	the university promoted positive visibility for the school partnership in the local community.	35 = 48 – 13 [36, 76]	32 = 49 – 17 [45, 60]	27 = 36 – 9 [56, 75]	29 = 44 – 15 [53, 68]
45/S4	in my opinion, teacher candidates placed in my school behaved in a professional and ethical manner.	44 = 76 – 32 [19, 61]	29 = 68 – 39 [30, 51]	36 = 75 – 39 [23, 54]	19 = 74 – 55 [19, 40]
63/S5	the university provided guidance for my school.	41 = 54 – 13 [33, 79]	43 = 57 – 14 [36, 66]	32 = 40 – 8 [55, 77]	19 = 40 – 21 [56, 68]
66/S5	my school benefited from consultants' participation who trained teachers.	24 = 42 – 18 [45, 66]	30 = 50 – 20 [44, 62]	20 = 36 – 16 [52, 69]	28 = 47 – 19 [49, 72]

Note: D = PDS%–CS%% stands for the percentage of *Yes* responses from PDS teachers minus the percentage of *Yes* responses from the CS teachers, which is represented by the letter D. All differences in percentages were statistically significant with alpha equal to .05 with the larger proportion always in favor of the PDSs. The pair of numbers in brackets, [PDS_U%, CS_U%], stands for the percentage of *Unsure* responses from the PDS teachers followed by the percentage of *Unsure* responses from the CS teachers.

focus above was on the differences in percentages of *Yes* responses between the PDS teachers and the CS teachers, it is of interest to see the actual percentages from which the differences were computed in order to judge the effect size; thus, percentages of *Yes* responses for PDS teachers (PDS$_Y$%) and CS (CS$_Y$%) teachers are reported. Also, in Table 5.3, percentages of *Unsure* responses are given for PDSs (PDS$_U$%) and CSs (CS$_U$%). When interpreting some of the items on the fidelity survey, we noted that each PDS may have had some interns and professors working within the school from other universities that were not in our PDS partnership. One can see in Table 5.3 the large number of items from the collaboration standard which contributed to it being the standard which showed the most difference in *Yes* responses between the PDS and CS teachers in Table 5.2.

Each item above was consistently statistically significant across all four years, providing a pattern which indicates support for PDS and helps control for Type I error rate. Also, many of the statistically significant results had observed p-values less than .001, which provides protection against increased Type I error by reducing the likelihood of an incorrect decision regarding statistical significance.

As can be seen in Table 5.3, the magnitude of the changes in *Yes* responses ranged from 59% difference between PDSs and CSs to 15%. The unweighted mean of these differences across the four years is 30.6%. The fact that the PDS partnership brought forth consistent changes in favor of the PDSs on these items over the four years is very supportive of the partnership.

When asking for teacher perceptions of the NCATE PDS standards, sometimes the teacher may not have the opportunity to observe the activity, and this should be considered when interpreting the item results. For example, item 36 asks: "During the last year, the university collaboratively coordinated the placement of teacher candidates in my school." To take into account the fact that some teachers may not know whether or not this activity occurred in their school, we included the *Unsure* response category on the fidelity survey. For example, Table 5.3 shows that in year one for item 36, 41% of the PDS teachers responded *Yes* and only 16% of the CS teachers said *Yes*. However, 46% of the PDS teachers were *Unsure* if there was collaboratively coordinated placement in contrast to 66% of the CS teachers.

The percentages of *No* responses can be calculated for any cell in Table 5.3. Due to the fact that there were only three response categories and the Internet survey was designed not to allow respondents to skip items, the percentage of *No* responses can be calculated by taking 100% minus the percentage of *Yes* responses plus the percentage of *Unsure* responses. For example, for item 36 in year one discussed above, the percentage of *No* responses for PDS was 13% and the percentage of *No* responses for CS was 18%.

We can also learn from non-significant results, and so we have provided the four items which meet the following criteria: no percentage of endorsement was more than 35% across all four years or there was a statistically significant difference of percentages in favor of CS teachers. These results are presented in Table 5.4.

Item three did not show significant differences because, although we started focusing more on action research as the PDS project moved forward across the years, there were still only a few teachers in each school who participated in action research studies. Most likely, still fewer teachers disseminated action research results due to the fact that participating in action research was typically not a job requirement of classroom teachers. Furthermore, this item also illustrates the breadth of PDS activities and brings forth the issue of the extent to which all teachers in the school are involved. Thus, an evaluation of this item might result in setting a much lower percentage as a target in comparison to other items. This type of item specific target or goal setting is the type of decision that a partnership might con-

TABLE 5.4 Differences in Percentages of *Yes* Responses for Teachers from Comparison and PDS Schools for Selected Items which Illustrate Aspects of Various Standards

Item No./ Stand.	Item	Year 1	Year 2	Year 3	Year 4
	During the last year...	$D = PDS_Y\% - CS_Y\%$ $[PDS_U\%, CS_U\%]$			
3/S1	I disseminated my action research findings beyond the PDS partnership (e.g., presented at professional conferences, published in professional journals).	$-9 =$ $12 - 21$ $[18, 18]$	$-7 =$ $16 - 23$ $[15, 8]$	$3 =$ $16 - 13$ $[19, 14]$	$-5 =$ $10 - 15$ $[14, 17]$
6/S1	knowledge gained through seminars, committees, or study groups in my school were used to inform practice.	$-9 =$ $75 - 84$ $[15, 5]$	$1 =$ $81 - 80$ $[10, 10]$	$-17 =$ $68 - 85$ $[13, 7]$	$14 =$ $84 - 70$ $[13, 15]$
10/S1	I participated in a cross-career professional learning community.	$5 =$ $26 - 21$ $[8, 8]$	$-1 =$ $32 - 33$ $[8, 5]$	$6 =$ $27 - 21$ $[15, 9]$	$12 =$ $29 - 17$ $[11, 4]$
30/S2	faculty at my school explored the possible constraints of the university partnership.	$15 =$ $26 - 11$ $[56, 63]$	$19 =$ $32 - 13$ $[51, 46]$	$4 =$ $17 - 13$ $[65, 70]$	$14 =$ $27 - 13$ $[59, 64]$

Note: $D = PDS_Y\% - CS_Y\%$ stands for the percentage of *Yes* responses from PDS teachers minus the percentage of *Yes* responses from the CS teachers, which is represented by the letter D. All differences of proportions in this table were not statistically significant at alpha equal .05 except Item 6 for year 3 where the difference (–17) was statistically significant in favor of the teachers from the Comparison Schools. The pair of numbers in brackets, $[PDS_U\%, CS_U\%]$, stands for the percentage of *Unsure* responses from the PDS teachers followed by the percentage of *Unsure* responses from the CS teachers.

sider. If most teachers should be involved in a PDS activity, then such a goal raises the question of the delivery method(s) a partnership might use to accomplish this target.

Except for item six in year three, from a classical hypothesis testing viewpoint, there is no evidence that the reported differences are other than zero in Table 5.4. Item six also illustrates that if there is no statistically significant difference, it does not necessarily imply that this aspect of a standard is not met. As seen in this item, the general trend is that approximately 70% to 80% of the teachers in both CSs and PDSs perceived gaining knowledge through seminars, committees, or study groups.

To help interpret the results in Table 5.4, we note that items which begin with "I" are asking about the individual teacher's activities, beliefs, or values in contrast to items which do not begin with "I," which ask for the teacher's perceptions of activities, beliefs, or values within his/her school. Thus, item ten is asking about an individual's participation in cross career learning communities, whereas item 30 ("During the last year, faculty at my school explored the possible constraints of the university partnership.") is asking an individual's perception of school level activities.

In general, we observed that after the first year of PDS implementation, according to the items on the survey, the endorsement of the presence of PDS activities, beliefs, and values essentially remained somewhat the same across the four years. Each item only measured the *presence* of a PDS activity, belief, or value and not its intensity. To investigate this issue further, we ran a two between factor multivariate analysis of variance as a guide to see if there were differences in means across years. One factor was PDS versus CS, and the other factor had four levels, one for each year of implementation.

We created one scale for each of the five standards to serve as dependent variables in the multivariate analysis of variance for a total of five scales. Each scale was constructed by adding the proportions of *Yes* responses of the items assigned to the scale based on the content of the items; consequently, this analysis included the responses to all 67 items in the fidelity survey. Before running the multivariate analysis of variance, we calculated coefficient alpha reliabilities for the five scales. All five reliabilities were at least .80 with some in the .90s. The results of the multivariate analysis of variance indicated a statistically significant difference for the PDS versus CS factor ($\Lambda = .84$, $p < .001$), but no significant difference across years ($\Lambda = .97$, $p = .32$), and no significant interaction between PDS versus CS factor and the year factor ($\Lambda = .99$, $p = .99$). For the PDS versus CS factor, follow-up F-tests to compare PDS to CS means for each of the five scales separately resulted in each scale showing a statistically significant difference ($p < .001$ for each scale). For the year factor, the multivariate analysis of variance essentially supported our contention that there was not a change in the *pres-*

ence of implementation as *perceived* by teachers across years based scales that consisted of the items assigned to the standards.

As previously mentioned, the intensity of a particular aspect of the PDS partnership, as reflected by a dichotomously scored item, was not assessed and may have increased across the years. Also, some of our changes which we implemented in PDSs in the later years would have only initially affected a small number of teachers. Thus, most likely these changes would not have shown up to any large extent on the fidelity survey in terms of the percentages of *Yes* responses from PDS teachers.

WHAT WE LEARNED

We believe that the NCATE PDS standards helped establish beneficial ways in which a clinical teacher education partnership between universities and schools can be focused. Thus, we were pleased that through our PDS project implementation, a higher percentage of PDS teachers perceived the presence of items measuring activities, beliefs, and values indicative of these standards than CS teachers. More specifically, in the contrasts using the 67 items on the fidelity survey over the four years, 45% of the contrasts favored the PDS teachers. Sixteen of the 67 items showed a statistically significant difference between PDS teachers and CS teachers in the first year of implementation and maintained statistically significant differences for the next three years. Thus, the PDS activities, beliefs, and values measured by these items persisted over four years.

Although many of the items showed significant differences, in some cases there was room for even higher endorsement. Whether or not a higher level of endorsement should be sought is a decision for the partnership. A target level of endorsement for an item could be set at the beginning of a year as a guide for program implementation.

We wrote items aligned to the NCATE PDS standards but also tailored some of the items to unique emphases in our PDS project. All of these items contributed to some *information need* for the project within the framework of the standards. For example, the low endorsement of action research by PDS teachers was responsible for us developing Anchor Action Research and mini-grants for PK–12 teachers and university professors to conduct action research (see Chapter 7).

The practical import of the decision making using the fidelity survey in conjunction with other pertinent information is that it can affect the way universities and school systems interact with each other in a PDS partnership. The decision making can also be facilitated by information gathered from sources such as focus groups, open-ended questions on surveys, face-to-face interviews, and classroom observations. We realize that as relationships develop, needs and goals change and partners can use data such as that available from a fidelity study to prompt consideration and analysis of changing initiatives over time.

The PDS Differential Implementation Fidelity Inventory we developed and used in our survey has implications for research regarding PDS implementations and the NCATE PDS standards. Given the unique nature of PDS relationships and the fact that individual partnerships determine the information they might need, we suggest that an item pool be developed continuously. In our study, an example of a particular PDS activity which we desired information about was cross career learning communities; thus, we created an item "During the last year, I participated in a cross-career professional learning community." Not all PDS partnerships would necessarily desire to spend available teacher time on this item in a survey, or the item may not be appropriate for a specific PDS. The sharing of and contributing to an item pool for use across PDS partnerships in various locations could help provide some normative information about implementation and might even lead toward a small set of common items which most PDSs would desire to use. Ultimately, through such an evolution, the fidelity survey might provide empirical data for validity studies which relate items or small sets of items on the same activity, belief, or value to other criteria such as student achievement, increased multicultural instruction, or teacher retention. In such a way, we could work together to establish a meaningful instrument which would enable those involved in clinical teacher education to understand the ways in which their collaborations reflect the standards set forth by NCATE as a model for school-university partnerships.

REFERENCES

Abdal-Haqq, I. (1998). *Professional development schools: Weighing the evidence.* Thousand Oaks, CA: Corwin Press.

Bickman, L. (1987). The functions of program theory. In L. Bickman (Ed.), *Using program theory in evaluation* (pp. 5–18). San Francisco: Jossey-Bass.

Bond, G.R. (1991). Variations in an assertive outreach model. *New Directions in Mental Health Sciences, 52,* 65–80.

Book, C. L. (1996). Professional development schools, In J. Sikula, T. Buttery, & E. Guyton (Eds.), *Handbook of research on teacher education* (2nd ed., pp. 194–210). New York: Macmillan.

Campoy, R.W. (2000). *A professional development school partnership: Conflict and collaboration.* Westport, CT: Bergin and Garvey.

Darling-Hammond, L., & McLaughlin, M. (1995). Policies that support professional development in an era of reform. *Phi Delta Kappan, 76,* 597–605.

Durlak, J. (1998). Why program implementation is important. *Journal of Prevention & Intervention in the Community, 17*(2), 5–18.

Dusenbury, L., Brannigan, R., Falco, M., & Lake, A. (2004). An exploration of fidelity of implementation in drug abuse prevention among five professional groups. *Journal of Alcohol and Drug Education, 27*(3), 4–20.

Elias, M. J. (1997). Reinterpreting dissemination of prevention programs as widespread implementation with effectiveness and fidelity. In R. P. Weissberg, T. P. Gullotta, R. L. Hampton, B. A. Ryan, & G. A. Adams (Eds.), *Establishing preventative services* (pp. 253–289). Thousand Oaks, CA: Sage.

Freeman, D. (1998). From here: A synthesis of the Chicago discussions on PDS standards. In M. Levin (Ed.), *Designing standards that work for professional development schools* (pp. 111–129). Washington, DC: National Council for Accreditation of Teacher Education.

Gresham, F.M. (1989). Assessment of treatment integrity in school consultation and prereffral intervention. *School Psychology Review, 18,* 37–50.

Gresham, F., MacMillan, D. L., Beebe-Frankenberger, M. B., & Bocian, K. M. (2000). Treatment integrity in learning disabilities intervention research: Do we really know how treatments are implemented? *Learning disabilities research and practice, 15,* 198–205.

Levin, M., & Churins, E.J. (1999). Designing standards that empower professional development schools. *Peabody Journal of Education, 74*(3&4), 178–208.

Meyer, A., Miller, S., & Herman, M. (1993). Balancing the priorities of evaluation with the priorities of the setting: A focus on positive youth development programs in school settings, *Journal of Primary Prevention, 14,* 95–113.

National Council for Accreditation of Teacher Education. (2001). *Standards for professional development schools.* Washington, DC: Author.

Petersilia, J. (1990). Conditions that permit intensive supervision. *Crime and Delinquency, 36*(1), 126–145.

Shadish, W., Cook, T., & Campbell, D. (2002). *Experimental and quasi-experimental designs for generalized causal inference.* Boston, MA: Houghton Mifflin Company.

Tractman, R. (1998). The NCATE professional development school study: A survey of 28 PDS sites. In M. Levine (Ed.), *Designing standards that work for professional development schools* (pp. 81–109). Washington, DC: National Council for Accreditation of Teacher Education.

CHAPTER 6

INTEGRATING INQUIRY IN CLINICAL TEACHER EDUCATION INITIATIVES ACROSS A PDS NETWORK

Donna Adair Breault
Northern Kentucky University

Chara Haeussler Bohan, Teresa Fisher, and Joyce E. Many
Georgia State University

Historically in the research on clinical teacher education in professional development schools (PDS), you can find limited attention devoted to inquiry as a *focus* of the partnerships (Berry, Boles, Edens, Nissenholtz, & Trachtman, 1996; Galassi, et al, 1999; Goodlad, 1988). Teacher educators and scholars, however, do underscore the value of making connections across theory, research, and practice in PDS sites (Darling-Hammond, 2005). University and school faculties are encouraged to collaborate with interns on reading, researching, and discussing their own efforts to answer problems unique to their sites (Lemlech, Hertzop-Foliar, & Hackl, 2005; Whitford, 2005). In addition, King's research (2002) documents that professional de-

Clinical Teacher Education, pages 93–115
Copyright © 2011 by Information Age Publishing
All rights of reproduction in any form reserved.

velopment can promote systematic school-wide inquiry and that such inquiry can lead to important changes in beliefs and practices.

Consistent with this literature on the importance of inquiry, we argue that inquiry should be at the *heart* of any clinical teacher education partnership between a university and partner schools. Inquiry should be the focus of the teacher education program, and that focus should permeate the experiences within the PDS. Similarly, the Holmes Group (1986) contends that a culture of inquiry provides stakeholders in school-university partnerships with the capacity to create a culture that values each participant's work, forges professional identities, and establishes identities through which collaboration can occur. Smylie, Bay, and Tozer (1999) underscore that inquiry must be a critical component of teacher education and the collaboration between universities and schools if teachers are to be agents of change. An inquiry-focused teacher preparation experience encourages pre-service teachers to accept the uncertainty of their work, to see the social consequences of their efforts, and to understand that teaching is more fluid and dynamic and requires collective problem solving by all stakeholders.

So what is an inquiry-focused clinical teacher education partnership? Given the range of images that have been presented in terms of "inquiry" or "reflection" in teacher education, (Smyth, 1992; Valli, 1993; Zeichner & Liston, 1996) we believe that it is critical to clearly articulate what we see as inquiry and offer a framework of necessary conditions for inquiry in our analysis of the partnerships within our institution. We use Dewey's theory of inquiry as the basis for our own characterization of inquiry in teacher education, and with this in mind, we believe partnerships should create educative experiences for pre-service and in-service teachers that promote growth in understanding, build community, and support democratic principles (Dewey, 1933, 1938).

Our image of inquiry is consistent with Rogers' (2002) characterization of reflective thinking in teacher education. Using Dewey as a basis for her work, Rogers argues that reflection involves making meaning based on experiences, how those experiences connect, and how they culminate into a larger understanding and response to society itself. In addition, reflection involves systematic inquiry within an engaged community for the sake of growth for one's self and for the community. When you consider the key concepts and principles emerging from both the PDS research and the accreditation rhetoric regarding partnerships—simultaneous renewal; learning communities; systematic examination of practice; professional growth among students, teachers, and professors; and concerns about diversity and equity—it is easy to see how a framework for inquiry inspired by Dewey can inform the work of professional development schools.

MOVING TO INQUIRY-FOCUSED CLINICAL TEACHER EDUCATION INITIATIVES IN PDS SCHOOLS

To illustrate our movement toward inquiry-focused clinical teacher education, next we present three stories from our PDS network. First, Joyce E. Many, an associate dean and member of the PDS design team, shares the project's steps to move the 15 collaborating schools in the PDS network toward an inquiry focus. In the second story, Teresa Fisher, a former PDS teacher who is now a university clinical faculty member, talks about her efforts within in-service professional development courses to help ESOL teachers across an elementary, middle, and high school cluster of PDS schools integrate inquiry into their curriculum and school culture. And finally, Chara Haeussler Bohan shares her experiences with integrating inquiry through the collaborative work at the high school PDS site where she serves as the PDS university coordinator.

Inquiry Across A PDS Network: Collaboration-Wide Efforts To Move To An Inquiry Focus

Our PDS collaborative network began with the involvement of five school systems and over 15 elementary, middle, and secondary schools. Like most clinical teacher education initiatives, our work was grounded in long-term partnerships with districts that had worked with us previously through involvements in field experiences, student teaching placements, and professional development opportunities. Our work together as PDS partners was initially framed around conversations juxtaposing the NCATE PDS standards and each individual site's school improvement plans. In this way, we hoped to integrate the PDS movements' focus on pre-service and in-service teacher development, on inquiry focusing on improving professional practice, and on increasing student achievement (Abdal-Haqq, 1988) with the unique needs and interest of each collaborating partner. In the initial years of our grant supported work, we worked hard to increase collaboration across university and school sites. We saw an increase in field-based courses with opportunities for school-based faculty to serve as guest lecturers or team-teachers; we increased the number of content-specific cohorts of student teachers in schools; and we altered teacher preparation programs in light of on-going discussions to respond to recommendations for year-long placements, use of new models for supervision, and site-based college course work for PDS teachers. We also had research initiatives focusing on the overall-PDS network's impact on student achievement and specific research projects ongoing at individual sites. As we moved into our third year of the partnership, however, we were particularly aware of the concerns in the literature regarding the tendencies of some partnerships to treat varying PDS activities (i.e., teacher preparation and development, student achievement, and/or research on teaching and learning) as distinct and separate initiatives. We wanted to avoid the grocery list mentality where PDS partner schools choose from these functions the one(s) in which they wish to concentrate, a tendency Levine and Churrin underscore as a major obstacle to PDS development. We believed inquiry to be the heart of the process through which PDS initiatives are integrated and become mutually shaping. Therefore, we set forth a set of experiences whereby the partners in our PDS network examined the importance of site-based inquiry and how such inquiry could inform the overall functioning of the clinical teacher education initiatives in a school.

First, we brought together university coordinators and faculty from the university and school-site coordinators and PDS site administrators from four of the districts with whom we work for a network-wide workshop focusing on inquiry. We began with a general introduction of the importance of inquiry in the teacher education literature. Beth Pendergraft of Augusta State University provided an overview of her university/school partnership in which PDS schools conduct site-based inquiries every five to six years as part of a school's reflection and renewal process and highlighted one school's efforts to examine their process of providing special education through inclusion (Pendergraft, 2007).

Next, school and university faculty from elementary, middle school, and secondary school sites reflected on their beliefs regarding the advantages of school–based inquiry. At the elementary level, participants stressed that inquiry study could provide teacher empowerment, shared responsibility, equality across voices, and could boost morale. These PDS faculty recognized the importance of problem solving in addressing goals related to personal, professional, and community growth and felt an asset of site-based inquiry was the ability to draw on resources from across the staff, community, and university. In such ways, the elementary participants felt inquiry could facilitate the school as a learning community where staff feels connected and vested, where a sense of professionalism is enhanced, and where student achievement is improved.

The middle-school PDS site and university coordinators, teachers, and administrators recognized the value of inquiry for concentrating on and potentially finding solutions related to grass roots issues and problems. Inquiry was seen as a vehicle for implementing change at the school level. The middle-school participants noted the importance of the inquiry process as bringing together both teachers and administrators in collaboration and personal reflection, and they underscored that such a process results in the enhancement of the learning environment for not only teachers but students as well. This group also stressed the sense of community that could result in site-based inquiry and underscored their belief that such inquiry could have a direct effect on instruction.

The educators participating in the group discussions at the secondary level felt the strength of site-based inquiry was that such a process looks at school-based issues and helps schools make real life connections to theories. This group stressed the notion of using data-driven decisions that could improve student learning. They also noted that undertaking such inquiries in their PDSs could build trust and improve relationships.

After considering the advantages of emphasizing site-based inquiry in our PDS initiatives, participants then met both with other educators teaching at similarly leveled schools (elementary, middle, and high schools across different systems) and with educators in their own school systems from schools in their cluster (feeder schools aligned from elementary to high school) to discuss possibilities for PDS inquiries and challenges to implementing such inquiries. Educators shared current projects and also brainstormed ways to identify school-wide issues that might be addressed. We believed it was critically important that we not only offer opportunities for faculty to conceive of the possibility but that we also consider what we might need to do as a group to sustain and facilitate an inquiry focus.

Several recommendations were made by the participants across various groups. One set of faculty recommended the creation of a school-wide survey to reveal possible inquiry topics. They noted the survey results could then be grouped and prioritized. A second recommendation was to solicit topics for inquiry through collaborative planning or from the school leadership team as part of the school improvement plan. This would involve the current infrastructure within schools but would also create a culture of inquiry where problem solving based on data and related steps for improvement were encouraged. A third recommendation was framed in light of participants' awareness that faculty can often feel over-worked and overburdened. This group recommended that use of the term "inquiry" might not be presented initially in order to prevent teachers from feeling they have to do another "activity" or "more work." Rather, the participants recommended that teachers simply be asked about issues or concerns. Next, efforts should be made to collect and analyze information systematically and then to address these issues with responsive action without labeling the process an "inquiry" activity. This group recognized the importance of *doing inquiry* whether or not the process was explicitly labeled as such. A final recommendation was that university coordinators and site coordinators could lead PDS faculty in the same process of considering the advantages of school-based inquiry, possible topics, and challenges as a way to encourage and stimulate the inquiry process.

In the spring after the PDS inquiry workshop, the PDS design team issued a call for anchor action research mini-grants. Through this initiative, university faculty and public school faculty were supported in the implementation of inquiry projects focusing on instructional interventions that led to school achievement. As a result, ten inquiry projects were funded for the subsequent school year. The PDS participants involved in the projects presented the results of their research to at the end of year four's PDS retreat, thus stimulating additional interest in how site-based inquiry could inform and shape instruction, teacher preparation, and student achievement. In such a way, we are working to fully integrate inquiry as a driving force behind the PDS initiatives in our schools. Plans were then made to continue mini-grant funding in year five of our grant.

Inquiry Within A Professional Development Initiative: A Look At One System's PDS ESOL Endorsement

In the context of professional development for in-service teachers in PDS schools, inquiry provides an opportunity for educators to engage in meaningful and purposeful collaboration in order to explore and address specific aspects of pedagogical and professional interest. Through the process of inquiry, teachers are empowered as they not only explore issues of concern but also collaboratively reconsider their own ways of being and teaching within the support of a learning community. In this section, we will describe the way in which Teresa Fisher, a PDS teacher who became a clinical faculty member at the university, worked to integrate inquiry into the professional development offered to ESOL PDS teachers. In the second year of our partnership, we offered a year long ESOL endorsement to teachers in a cluster of PDS schools. Ten teachers gathered on a bi-weekly basis for five hours of instruction, conversation, and collaboration regarding the teaching and learning of English as a Second Language. During the first hour of our first class meeting, I (Teresa Fisher) realized that the secondary PDS teachers (the vast majority of participants in the coursework) were very troubled by the extraordinarily low graduation rate of English Language Learners (ELLs) at their school. Their high school has the highest percentage of English Language Learners and economically disadvantaged students of any high school in the southeast and has a stated drop out rate of 52%. Based on their own records, however, the teachers were certain that percentage was in fact a gross underestimation. Teachers explained that every week they lose at least one student who has decided to drop out of school. As this concern became a focus of our conversations, these educators began to realize that there was great deal more that individual teachers and the school in general could do to support the personal and academic success of these students. Although educational policies, multiple mandates, and decreased professional autonomy often leave teachers feeling as if they cannot significantly change their practice or their school context, within our PDS endorsement experience these teachers engaged in a year-long collective inquiry surrounding the school-wide concern of student failure. This professional development journey, driven by teacher concern and problem solving, led to a significant transformation in the ways that teachers envisioned their own roles. This process was also liberating for many of the teachers as they began to recognize their own power to transform practices, policies, and procedures on a classroom and on a school wide level.

Though the explicit purpose of the ESOL four-course endorsement was for these teachers to become better able to serve ELLs in the context of their content area classrooms, a more overarching goal of promoting the personal and academic success of all students was implicit in our work. At the beginning of our journey together, all teachers believed they could improve their practice. While many of the teachers had considered the ways that the societal, economic and circumstantial pressures shaped the lives of students, few had considered the ways that some of these issues could be addressed at school and in their own classrooms. These teachers always had a high level of commitment and had advocated for many of their individual students through strong personal relationships. However, they had not, for the most part, considered ways in which they could reconceptualize and advocate for those students on a broader, more school/community-wide level. The long term engagement and collaboration of teachers who were serving the same student population proved to be a very powerful tool for professional change and growth.

During the first semester of the ESOL endorsement coursework, teachers interviewed their students and asked the students to identify a social issue they felt to be detrimental to their academic success. As a result, the teachers uncovered a range of issues that their students cited as reasons for leaving school. Teachers found multiple and often compounding factors, such as the need for young mothers to have decent care for their young children, the effects of testing on ELLs who have had limited formal or consistent schooling, and the personal and financial difficulties of many students who came to the United States alone, who are supporting themselves by trying to hold down a full time job after school, and who still attend the full traditional day of high school. Other issues that were explored were the increased involvement of students in gang-related activities, the lack of meaningful after school engagements available for students, and the limited access to books and linguistically appropriate literacy materials.

Next, as part of the course experiences, the teachers researched, interviewed, discussed, and took a stance on specific potential solutions to these problems that interfered with student success. They supported their stance with student comments and research. Portions of multiple class sessions were spent discussing the issues and brainstorming ways to best meet the needs of students. Though this was a significant portion of the coursework, very few specific parameters were set, other than the fact that we needed to consider alternatives, both on a macro (systemic policy) and a micro (classroom and school context) level that we would actively put into motion. This call to action moved our inquiries from the theoretical to the pragmatic as real action was taken to bring some of these "dreams" into fruition. Through this process, teachers questioned the obvious and reconceptualized possibilities, shared resources, and collectively considered potential courses of action that could be taken both individually and as a group.

The fact that throughout the four ESOL endorsement courses I was the instructor and the teachers remained an intact cohort provided an opportunity for a long term community of practice to be constructed in which common issues and concerns could be raised. In addition, though the larger issues of the personal and academic achievement of ELLs (and of all students) was the focus, there was significant flexibility as teachers chose to explore the issue about which they were most concerned and impassioned. Although all of the teachers were working to understand aspects of schooling and society that contributed to the academic failure of their students, the wide range of topics explored through teacher projects reflected the different interests, emphasis, and concerns of the different teachers working in the same school. These issues were often ones that individual teachers had struggled with and pondered for a long time. The year-long analysis led to recognition of the absolute complexity of student lives and to a more comprehensive and multidimensional understanding of ways of being and "doing" school that could be reshaped to best meet the needs of the students served. Through our multifaceted investigation, we mutually encouraged each other, collaborated, shared resources and connections, and critically examined concerns as we collectively pondered potential actions. We not only considered the issues, but also asked ourselves what *we* could do to ameliorate them. The specific and shared context, the multiple lenses of potential change, the collaborative relationships built by the teachers through the inquiry process, and particularly the stories of individual students were the driving forces of this process and the key to its success.

Our inquiries surrounding social justice resulted in consideration of multiple layers of personal responsibility. The participating teachers transformed their classrooms, schools, and community in many varied and remarkable ways. One teacher worked to inform students, families, and teachers of the multiple (and under-publicized) options for alternative schooling with flexible hours that would allow students who had long work hours to successfully complete high school. A second teacher received a grant to create family libraries and books on tape for young ELL students and their families, providing them with literacy and linguistic support in English. Another teacher proposed and led a professional development experience for teachers to help them recognize gang markings and signs that were present in their classrooms but that teachers did not know how to identify. He was specifically passionate about supporting those kids who were involved in gangs and providing alternative supportive relationships for them and believed that if teachers did not recognize what was going on, they would be less likely to provide the extra support and encouragement these students needed. Yet another teacher became very engaged in an organization working to provide alternatives for NCLB reauthorization that would more equitably serve ELLs and economically disadvantaged students. She statistically analyzed the state's "End of Course Tests" for her subject matter and demonstrated that the higher the number of ELLs and economically disadvantaged students served by a school, the fewer students passed the test. She framed a powerful argument about educational equity, the accountability movement, and the "pushing out" of minority populations from high schools. As a result of her inquiry, this teacher decided to apply to a Ph.D. program in educational policy studies to become a more able to advocate for the students and families she serves.

Teachers were also able to work together on topics of interest. One group of teachers was very concerned about the students in their classrooms who were expectant mothers. These young women explained in their interviews that they were going to have to drop out when they became mothers because there was no appropriate and affordable childcare available. As a result of the inquiry project, these PDS teachers went to the administration and the school board with a proposal for establishing, in collaboration with our university, an Early Childhood Education Center for their school site. The school is likely to receive 16 million dollars of local tax money, and these teachers have volunteered to be on the committee to determine how these funds might best be spent. The proposed early learning center would be a high quality childcare facility housed within the school building and would provide a location for students and teachers to bring their children for enriching and educational opportunities during the academic day. The proposal under consideration includes a college credit course in early childhood development that would take place in the center where interested students could learn about early childhood development, improve child care and parenting skills, and receive academic credit.

Inquiry-based clinical teacher education partnerships should have a significant purpose beyond themselves. Indeed, this process served to inform, reform, and transform the ways of teaching, learning, and living for many, if not all, of the participants in this process. Teachers completed the ESOL endorsement with an ability to teach strategically and intentionally to meet the linguistic, literacy, and content area needs of the English language learners in their classrooms. Equally important, they also gained the confidence, knowledge, and disposition for using their own professional voice to advocate for the students, families, and communities they serve. They had an increased awareness of the importance of the "outside of school lives" of their students. They had moved past an individual and collective *dreaming* that things could be better and had researched, conceptualized, and enacted solutions to some of these issues. Through the inquiry process, teachers made individual changes in their own practices and had in many ways (re) conceptualized schooling. Teachers joined organizations, wrote to and met with policy makers and worked to educate others within their circle of influence about the importance of educational equity. The teachers themselves were empowered and left more confident in their ability to reshape their world, community, and classrooms into more just places.

If we, in teacher education, infuse inquiry into our work with current and future educators, teachers will be more willing and have more of the tools to trouble the obvious, to question that which is in place, and to consider alternative actions and processes in order to meet students where they are and provide experiences and educative opportunities that foster success, academically and personally, for students. It is only through this emancipatory stance toward education that teachers will be able to go into the often prescriptive environments of schools today and question, consider, reflect, collaborate, and transform the ways of being that too often result in limited success for students in high-needs schools.

Inquiry At The School Site Level: A Look At One Secondary PDS

In order to support a culture of inquiry, clinical teacher education partnerships must demonstrate that they are collective in nature. Evidence of a collective culture includes communication, time and interaction, change and choice, reciprocity, and reflection on personal relationships. At the PDS high school where I (Chara Haeussler Bohan) was a university liaison, we had many examples of a collective culture. Communication occurred routinely among the university faculty, school administrators, and teachers. For example, I attended the site's weekly leadership team meetings, where together the leaders worked to find solutions to concerns in the school. The meetings served to inform, reform, and sometimes transform. At the meetings, school events were announced, such as sporting events, drama performances, science fairs, and open houses. As the university liaison, I was responsible for working with all the student teaching interns across subject area disciplines. In addition, creating a workspace for partnership activities facilitated communication. My PDS site also provided a room for university faculty and interns to meet and work. Partnership activities occurred in this space regularly.

In addition, the collective partnership worked together to implement reform when problems were perceived. Our leadership team tried to improve the daily class schedule, to voice objection to administrative changes imposed by the Superintendent's office, to assist students who struggle with end of course testing, to increase minority student participation in Advanced Placement Courses, to select avenues for professional development, and to find solutions to students who exhibit behavior problems. When communication could not happen in person, it occurred several times a week via electronic mail. A simple tool, email increased interaction between the school and university faculty. Both the quantity and quality of the time devoted to interactions among the school's stakeholders was easily facilitated by the widespread use of email as a communication device.

As the university PDS coordinator, I also joined the school faculty members to read and discuss education books and articles as part of professional development. Together, the partners shared resources to help support educative experiences. The faculty read Marzano, Pickering and Pollock's (2005) *Classroom Instruction that Works: Research Based Strategies for Increasing Student Achievement* to gain ideas for how to facilitate improved student learning. I also shared Hmelo-Silver's (2004) article on problem-based learning to provide research on instructional methods for teachers who wanted to learn new teaching strategies. In addition, school and university faculty attended Critical Friends professional development training and began implementing small, professional development communities of teachers within the school. Both the public school teachers and the university faculty benefitted from engagement in educative experiences, as the relationship helped to bridge the perceived gap between theory and practice.

The inquiry-based partnership between the university and my PDS site provided mutual educative experiences. One example was the collaborative effort I engaged in with the social studies department chair, an advanced placement (AP) psychology teacher, to investigate the use of primary source documents in her social studies classroom. The partnership led to the writing and award of an anchor action research mini-grant to support research in the classroom. The high quality of this educative experience helped both the high school teachers and the university faculty members understand and assess the value of using specific materials in classrooms. Through this collaborative experience, a new path for using primary source materials emerged. The AP psychology teacher began using the primary source documents book that was procured as part of the mini-grant as a remedial tool for her poor performing students. The result was that six of eight struggling students elevated their Pre-AP exam scores to a 3 or higher. As the work on this grant evolved, new paths of learning were created for both the teacher and myself as a researcher as we partnered together to explore classroom learning.

All the PDS schools in the network shared the purpose of helping students learn and improving student achievement. It was the guiding principle of our partnership work. Indeed, the federal government grant to support the PDS partnership was funded with the researchable goal of determining whether the partnership would lead to improved student achievement. Teachers, administrators, and university faculty worked together to achieve this shared goal. At the same time, not all members of our partnership necessarily exhibited the same beliefs about how improving student learning could be actualized. Context and participants are important to consider in order to understand why beliefs, values, and commitment to a shared purpose vary to a certain extent. Our school was situated in a suburb north of the city that could be described as a multifaceted urban environment. The community consisted of affluent and middle class homes situated near car dealerships, apartment complexes, gas stations, and strip malls. Our teachers reported that approximately half the students who lived in the surrounding neighborhood attended the public schools and the other half attended private schools. At the same time, our school was a charter school with a dual magnet program in Arts and Sciences which drew students from all over the county. The performing arts and the science magnet programs attracted students with tremendous artistic and/or logical abilities. There were also "neighborhood kids" who were sometimes depicted as struggling learners, and who comprised the majority of the students of minority racial/ethnic groups and low socio-economic status. There was a sizable ELL population, as well. The National Center for Education Statistics reported that for a recent school year our student body of 1,744 students was comprised of the following racial/ethnic categories: 767 black, 742 white, 115 Hispanic, 56 Asian, 3 American Indian (National Center for Education Statistics, 2006). Approximately, one-third of our students (525) qualified for free and reduced price lunch. In the hallway of the school hang approximately 60 flags that represent the various nations from which students hail, so the school was diverse in every sense of the word.

Although the teachers at our high school all wanted their students to succeed, they did not all agree on the means to achieve academic success. During the third year of our partnership, the principal asked department chairs how they were helping students who had not passed the state high school graduation test. Of the all of the departments, only one offered support, which was in the form of after school and/or weekend tutoring. The other department chairs reported that what was offered in class was sufficient, and that the problem rested with students who failed to attend class regularly. In order to assist students but ease the burden on the teachers, as the university liaison I arranged for the pre-service student teachers to assist with tutoring sessions during the class day. Some teacher objection remained, as students were pulled out of regular classes for test preparation drills, and cooperating teachers had to teach class rather than have their university interns available to provide instruction. Nonetheless, there were 157 students who had not passed a particular section (LA –15, math – 23, science – 75, SS – 38, writing – 6) of the state graduation test in February of that year who received assistance in the months that followed. In June, after the tutoring sessions and an opportunity to retest, the number dropped to 56 (LA – 5, math – 7, science – 27, SS – 14, writing – 3). With a new charter in place for the fourth year of the partnership, the high school faculty created year round learning labs during lunch to assist their struggling students. Now the tutoring sessions are a permanent feature of the school.

In order to make our PDS network actively work, university PDS coordinators like me committed to working at the partner schools one day a week. This commitment took different forms at different schools, depending on the needs and desires of the school. At my school, it meant attending weekly leadership meetings and helping to organize and guide tutoring sessions for students who failed some standardized testing measures. Our active partnership continued to grow over time. In the fourth year of our partnership, nine pre-service student teachers were placed in science, social studies, English, and counseling and there were several ESOL placements for shorter term field experiences, as well. Five university personnel came into the building to supervise the university interns, and as one of those five, I also came to the PDS once a week as the university liaison. Many of the public school personnel also benefited from the active relationship, as PDS faculty sought advanced degrees at our university and received scholarships as part of the partnership. In addition, a number of our pre-service teachers also gained employment at the school after completing their internship at the PDS site.

The purpose of our PDS partnership was to work together to help students achieve and assist teachers and university faculty to continue professional growth. The partnership served a significant purpose beyond itself through activities such as providing tutoring sessions, reading educational literature, establishing space in which to work, attending leadership meetings in order to collaboratively find solutions to school-wide and community concerns, working with student teacher interns to mentor future teachers, and writing grants in order to research the use of primary source documents. As the university liaison, I contributed first-hand in the actual school building to helping the partnership achieve its goals.

Of course, there was room for further growth. The impact on the larger metropolitan community was difficult to discern, and work to reform teacher education still lies ahead. Because the partnership is collective, exists within an educative experience, has a shared purpose, and remains active, the partnership can continue to thrive and work to achieve the goals of impact on the community and reform of teacher education. Indeed, as partners we hope to work on subsequent grants to accomplish the later two goals.

REFLECTIONS ON INQUIRY-FOCUSED CLINICAL TEACHER EDUCATION INITIATIVES

As illustrated in the above stories, Dewey's notion of inquiry served as the basis for our work. Specifically, we can identify five conditions of inquiry which are integrated within our clinical teacher education partnerships. We believe stakeholders need to create, support, and sustain these conditions in order for the relationship to be a reflective or inquiry-based partnership (Adair-Breault, 2004). First, inquiry-based partnerships are collective—creating a meaningful community that involves all stakeholders. Second, inquiry-based partnerships create and sustain educative experiences—all stakeholders within the partnership learn how to improve themselves and their school and community by virtue of being part of the partnership. Third, inquiry-based partnerships support a shared purpose—they seek common and meaningful outcomes from their work. Fourth, inquiry-based partnerships are active—they involve engaged relationships among the stakeholders. Finally, inquiry-based partnerships serve a significant purpose beyond themselves—their work not only improves the conditions for teacher preparation and in-service training, it also affects the school community in meaningful ways.

Clinical Teacher Education Communities of Inquiry Are Collective

First, we believe clinical teacher education partnerships that support a culture of inquiry are collective. The relationship between the school and the university creates a community of inquirers. As Dewey (1916) notes, democratic communities make knowing a public process. Communication among members of the community makes their shared experiences more meaningful. He notes, "Every individual has grown up, and always must grow up, in a social medium. His responses grow intelligent, or gain meaning simply because he lives and acts in a medium of accepted meanings and values." (p. 295)

A collective body of knowledge is formed when members of the community collectively explore consequences of actions, form hypotheses, and examine concepts and ideas. Thus, knowledge about teaching and learning within a clinical teacher education partnership becomes a collective and educative achievement. Relationships are formed where stakeholders in the partnership work together over time to better understand the educative process and how they can make a difference in their school by focusing on commonly shared goals.

We have identified a number of indicators for collective partnerships that demonstrate the degree to which they support inquiry. For example, communication is a critical indicator in such partnerships. At Chara Haeussler Bohan's PDS high school, she attends leadership meetings where agendas were shared, and email communication was frequent. Beyond enabling communication of information, clinical teacher education partnerships must also allow for transformative communication by creating spaces in which stakeholders can be open to possibilities together. Examples of such spaces in our partnerships include the anchor action research projects, and professional development course where the teachers of ELL students sought to take action to address student concerns. When educators within a PDS work toward greater possibilities within the partnership and their programs, then they are functioning within a state of inquiry that can respond to the complex nature of schooling and seek greater levels of understanding in the midst of that complexity.

In addition to communication, collective efforts between schools and universities need sustained and positive interaction. The amount of time participants can spend together and the nature of their interaction influence the degree to which inquiry can exist within the partnership. This interaction needs to involve authentic engagement—such as occurred in the three stories, where teachers and university faculty planned action research projects together, wrote grants together, developed new programs to serve students, and worked across systems to develop network initiatives.

In addition, inquiry-based partnerships also achieve collectivity through reciprocity. Communication and interaction among stakeholders may bring about change, but the degree to which a group of people working together in a clinical teacher education partnership support a culture of inquiry is contingent upon the degree to which the efforts are deliberate and mutual. Dewey (1954) argued that communities are formed as social and moral entities through deliberate efforts driven by mutually esteemed goals. This state of community, according to Dewey, takes time to develop. Clearly, in the three stories, inquiry efforts, whether they involved the use of primary source documents in a social studies classroom, the facilitation of teacher initiatives to assist ELL students, or the creation of network wide mini-grant programs, took time to develop.

Inquiry-Based Partnerships Exist Within Educative Experiences

According to Dewey, the aim of education is growth, and thus, educative experiences are those that offer the greatest potential for growth—the greatest likelihood that the student will increase his or her capacity for more learning. Shaker (2005) elaborates on Dewey's notion of growth, noting that truly educative experiences do not merely deposit a body of facts into the student. Instead, they enrich and animate the student's capacity to learn and his or her desire to change by virtue of what his or she has learned through experiences. We identified three indicators that help us discern the degree to which experiences within a PDS or other clinical teacher education partnerships are truly educative. We first considered continuity within pre-service and in-service teachers' experiences within a partnership—the degree to which theory and practice were connected within the current context. We also considered the degree to which stakeholders within a partnership engage in real problem solving, and the degree to which the efforts of the partnership create experiences that are consistent with the aims of the institutions and the partnership itself.

Clinical teacher education partnerships achieve continuity when they are able to create and support an organic connection between the work of the school and the work of the university. This connection helps stakeholders see the vital relationship between theory and practice. Partnerships that promote continuity provide experiences where pre-service teachers can better understand what it means to be a teacher by being a teacher—observing, planning, teaching, reflecting, and engaging in meaningful classroom research about teaching and learning. This image of continuity can also be seen in the hands-on opportunities interns at Chara's PDS high school experienced in working with students who were struggling to pass the high school end of course tests required in the core curriculum courses. At other sites, field-based courses (see Chapter 4) that enable direct connections between theory and practice further helped interns create bridges between what theories and research and lived-through clinical teacher education experiences in PDS schools.

While continuity between theory and practice in teacher education is important, clinical experiences in professional development schools also need to lead stakeholders to solve a problem or series of problems. Open-ended problem solving can widen the range of purposes within experience to reveal more vividly the conditions in which faculty, teachers and pre-service teachers operate and the possibilities their actions afford. Open problem solving is consistent with Dewey's (1929) notion of inquiry, and it is the kind of problem solving we seek in order to label an experience highly educative. Inquiry projects such as those framed by the ESOL teachers in their professional development sequence of courses with Teresa Fisher, exemplified this type of problem solving. Similarly, the site-based inquiry initiatives conceptualized by university and school faculty from across the PDS network, and later supported by the network's mini-grant program were also indicative of this educative approach. These projects also brought together participants around a shared purpose, a second characteristic of inquiry-based partnerships which we will discuss further in the section below.

Inquiry-Based Partnerships Have A Shared Purpose

In inquiry-based partnerships, the notion of purpose is extended to all stakeholders who are part of the community of inquiry. Dewey (1929) argued that a community exists only as far as its aims are established and clearly communicated. Common goals, beliefs, and assumptions guide its members. When a university and a public school choose to work together, they are creating a new community that did not exist prior to the agreement. Therefore, they must make sure they share a common set of beliefs and goals for the relationship to succeed and for the partnership to support intelligent action.

Research clearly indicates that the first condition for collaborative partnerships involves common normative ground (Dresher, Brulingame, & Fuhriman, 1985; Lieberman, Yolom, & Miles, 1973). For this to happen, partnerships should be formed and operated according to ideas that are bigger than mere state-level requirements for certification, and the commitment to larger ideas should be mutual. Stakeholders in clinical teacher education partnerships should have shared values and assumptions upon which the partnership is formed and through which it functions even if other values and beliefs may differ (Adair-Breault, 2005). For example, university professors may place a higher priority on the theoretical foundations of teaching than their school counterparts. This difference alone should not prevent stakeholders from working together. As Teitel (1992) and Galassi, White, Vesilind, and Bryan (2001) note in their PDS research, partnerships are able to achieve shared aims even if participants in the partnership do not always change their beliefs or priorities.

In inquiry-based partnerships, both the university and the school must agree upon their shared purposes. Finding common purposes can be a challenge given the different cultures within each institution. Slater (1996) addressed this issue with what she identified as a "class war" between universities and public schools. According to Slater, public schools are often trying to maintain their existing order and structures while universities are attempting to bring about change. She argued that reform is not possible as long as participants within a partnership maintain this division of purpose. Both the school and university must work together to understand the differences within their cultures, and with that understanding, work together to bring about positive change.

Our mission was to bring together university and public school educators to create an urban PDS network. We agreed that together our work would result in (a) increased production and retention of new teachers (especially underrepresented groups), (b) increased student achievement, and (c) professional renewal for all PDS participants. Beyond those expectations, however, we strove to create a partnership which was flexible enough to meet the conditions Dewey outlined as necessary conditions for a common sense of purpose to be established. First, aims must be determined by the participants rather than by external influences, and these choices should be based upon the unique opportunities within the relationship. In our partnerships, while the value of inquiry was discussed and facilitated at the network level, specific inquiry initiatives were site-based. School level projects were often determined by leadership teams, such as the one at Chara Haeusler Bohan's PDS high school site. Other inquiries were framed by university faculty and cooperating teachers working with interns in specific content areas (see TIP model, Chapter 7). The fact that projects were conceptualized and designed by collaborative partners who were the closest to the needs of the PDS ensured that a shared purpose existed.

To establish a shared purpose, Dewey (1929) also argued that goals between schools and universities should exist as tentative sketches, open to revision. Aims should guide action, not prescribe it. Further, aims should lead to an outcome, activity, or achievement. The aim itself is not the end to which PDS stakeholders ascribe. Rather, the act of achieving the aim is the ultimate desired outcome. When partners fail to make this distinction, they run the risk of separating ends and means. In our PDS approach, each site creates a plan for PDS activities based on each of the school's professional improvement plans. By working together, PDS educators consider the needs of the school and the available PDS resources (including monetary resources, people, and potential educator preparation programs) as they consider ways to involve university interns at the school. The university site coordinator, PDS coordinator, and the participating faculty work together to shape specific experiences that best meet the needs of both the public school students and the pre-service and in-service teachers. In such ways, the collaborative discussions create the synergy needed for effective collaboration, further strengthening the relationships and enabling the communication needed for a successful inquiry approach to clinical teacher education work. Such an approach to PDS work also contributes to a site's ability to be actively responsive to changing needs, another key element of inquiry-based partnerships.

Inquiry-Based Partnerships Are Active

According to Dewey (1929), "Action is the means by which a problematic situation is resolved." (p. 195) For their actions to remain consistent with

Dewey's notion of inquiry, we believe stakeholders within clinical teacher education partnerships must actively pursue change as their ultimate goal. Participants from both the public school and the university must be active participants in achieving the goals of the partnership. All stakeholders must take responsibility for bringing about change in both institutions, and this cannot happen without both getting involved in the operations of each institution.

However, Dewey offered a note of caution that is appropriate for clinical teacher education partnerships. He noted that actions should be thoughtful and purposeful, not rash. He pointed to the tendency of human nature to act too quickly. Instead, he argued that people should be patient and understand that many of their actions will not directly bring about change.

When stakeholders within clinical teacher education partnerships are actively committed to the messy change over time characteristic of a partnership, they are more likely to support one another and sustain the relationship over time. Realizing the scope of their endeavors, stakeholders are less likely to fall back upon mindless habits and prescriptive measures. In other words, active commitment to the complex work of a partnership decreases the likelihood of inertia—where ideas are accepted blindly or passively and work together becomes mechanical and automatic (Dewey, 1934).

Previous research on school-university relationships, however, indicates change does not necessarily occur for all stakeholders or for all programs and institutions within a partnership (Galassi et al., 2001; Teitel, 1992). Culture and disposition play an important role in the degree to which stakeholders in a partnership will change. In our PDS network, we have found that communication is of utmost importance for real change to occur. The participants most integrally involved in activities, such as the university coordinators, PDS coordinators, and design team members, are the most likely to be sensitive to changes which are occurring either systemically or in attitudes, dispositions, and levels of commitments of the participants. Network-wide discussions between university and PDS coordinators and our yearly retreat with participants help partners develop a common language and appreciate each other's perspectives. These PDS leaders must then work diligently to share these experiences with other teachers in the school site and faculty in the teacher education programs, to complete the circuit of information flow across the network.

Previous research (DeWitt et al., 1998) indicates that teacher educators who participated in a partnership thought that their own beliefs about teaching and learning were challenged through the experience. While changes may not result in the complete understanding or appreciation of one another or absolute commitment to all aims of the partnership (Silva, 2000), partners can move toward greater understanding and appreciation of the perspectives and aims of others. Working together can potentially increase the understanding and appreciation among school and university stakeholders (Brooks, 1996; Driskell & Salas, 1997). Increased understanding and appreciation provide the critical elements for more meaningful relationships. Further, the more meaningful partners' relationships are with one another, the more likely they will work together in positive ways to bring about change. Thus, the cycle supports a dynamic relationship among partners for significant change in the schools (Mebane & Galassi, 2003; Robinson & Darling-Hammond, 2005). At the same time, while collaborations like our PDS network can facilitate change, we also note that a broader purpose is served by our inquiry-based partnership as well. This final element is discussed in the section which follows.

Inquiry-Based Partnerships Serve A Significant Purpose Beyond Themselves

According to Dewey (1916), it is not enough that people are good; they must be good for something. Collectively serving a greater good is best described within his notion of democracy, and clinical teacher education partnerships can look to his notion of democracy as an ideal state in which they function. In essence, communities of inquiry should be democratic communities. Members of a democratic community are socially responsible for acting upon any conditions within the society in need of reform.

If we are to consider clinical teacher education partnerships as communities of inquiry, then we need to recognize that these communities are dynamic communities where members promote better habits in order to improve the quality of life for all. School-university partnerships should achieve some greater end than the building and maintenance of the relationship itself. The partnership has the potential to not only influence the preparation of future teachers, but also to support the professional growth of practicing teachers and teacher educators. The partnership may also find ways to serve the school and its community. When the teachers in our PDS network are supported in their efforts to find ways to meet the needs of the students and families in their school, they serve this broader purpose. By publicizing alternative school days to allow working students who must support their families to continue to attend schools, by developing family literacy programs, by creating child care opportunities to keep students in schools, school-university partners are going beyond the building of partnerships to making a difference in the school community. A larger purpose is also served when stakeholders research their practice, such as through site based inquiry projects, through which they may also influence the professional community with new findings regarding the preparation of teachers and the improved conditions for student learning.

We believe a commitment to inquiry-based partnerships contributes to the differences that PDS partnerships can make. As school and university inquiry-based partnerships expand, we need to both maintain and broaden our focus on the impact of such relationships. Research needs to continue to explore the degree to which pre-service teachers from PDSs are better prepared for planning, instruction, management, and assessment than their counterparts who are not part of a PDS (e.g., Castle, Fox, & Souder, 2006). Similarly, research such as that by Linek, Fleener, Fazio, Raines, and Klakamp (2003) focusing on how PDS schools result in statistically significant increases in student achievement is important. At the same time, we recognize, as Eisner (2001) has noted, that what we measure is what matters. While it is important and commendable that clinical teacher education models are making a difference in teacher preparation and student achievement, we believe future research should also consider the community created by a professional development school partnership and how the partnership impacts the quality of life for the students and their families within the community, as well as the vocational development and professionalization of practicing teachers and university faculty.

In conclusion, we believe, through inquiry focused collaborations, that the role of schools in a democratic society can be most fully realized. By collaboratively situating meaningful inquiry at the heart of clinical teacher education partnerships as described in this chapter, we work together as active members within a democratic community, as citizens who promote the common good (Dewey & Tufts, 1932). This inquiry model of education empowers both public school and university educators and demonstrates that we do, indeed, have a voice and the ability, both personally and collectively, to (re)invent the policies, processes and practices in place not only in classrooms, but also in the schools and communities in which we work.

REFERENCES

Abdal-Haqq, I. (1998). *Professional development schools: Weighing the evidence.* Thousand Oaks, CA: Corwin Press.

Adair-Breault, D. (2005). Van Gogh and Gauguin and impressions from Arles: Inquiry's potential within collegiality. *Educational Forum, 69,* 240–253.

Adair-Breault, D. (2004). Conditions of inquiry within school and university partnerships. In J. Guardarrama, Ramsey, J., & Nath, J. (Eds.), *Professional development school research* (pp. 29–46). Charlotte, NC: Information Age Publishing.

Berry, B., Boles, K., Edens, K., Nissenholtz, A., & Trachtman, R. (1996, June). *Inquiry and professional development schools.* Report for The National Center for Restructuring Education, Schools, and Teaching.

Brooks, C. L. (1996). Professional development schools. In J. Sikula (Ed.), *Handbook of research on teacher education* (pp. 194–210). New York: Macmillan.

Castle, S., Fox, R.K., & Souder, K. (2006). Do professional development schools (PDSs) make a difference?: A comparative study of PDS and non-PDS teacher candidates. *Journal of Teacher Education, 57*(1), 65–80.

Darling-Hammond, L., & Baratz-Snowden, J. (2005). *A good teacher in every classroom: Preparing the highly qualified teachers our children deserve.* San Francisco, CA: Jossey-Bass.

Dewey, J. (1916). *Democracy and education.* New York: Macmillan Publishing Company.

Dewey, J. (1929). *The sources of a science of education.* New York: Liveright Publishing Corporation.

Dewey, J. (1933). *How we think.* Boston: D.C. Heath and Company.

Dewey, J. (1934). *Art as experience.* New York: The Berkeley Publishing Company.

Dewey, J. (1938). *Logic: The theory of inquiry.* New York: Henry Holt Co.

Dewey, J. (1954). *The public and its problems.* Athens, OH: Ohio University Press.

Dewey, J., & Tufts, J. (1932). *Ethics* (2nd ed.). New York: Henry Holt and Company.

DeWitt, P., Birrell, J.R., Egan, M.W., Cook, P.F., Ostlund, M. F., & Young, J. R. (1998). Professional development schools and teacher educators' beliefs: Challenges and change. *Teacher Education Quarterly, 25*, 63–80.

Drescher, S., Burlingame, G., & Fuhrman, A. (1985). Cohesion: An odyssey in empirical understanding. *Small Group Behavior, 16*, 3–30.

Driskell, J. E., & Salas, E. (1997). Collective behavior and team performance human factors. In D. Russ-Eft, H. Preskill & C. Sleezer (Eds.), *Human resource development review: Research and implications* (pp. 277–288). Thousand Oak, CA: Sage Publications.

Eisner, E. (2001). What does it mean to say a school is doing well? *Phi Delta Kappan, 82*(5), 367–372.

Galassi, J. P., Brader-Araje, L., Brooks, L., Dennison, P., Jones, M. G., Mebane, D. J., Parrish, J., Richer, M., White, K., Vesiling, E. M., (1999). Emerging results from a professional development school: The McDougle-University of North Carolina collaborative inquiry partnership groups. *Peabody Journal of Education, 74*(3 & 4), 236–253.

Galassi, J. P., White, K. P., Vesilind, E. M., & Bryan, M. E. (2001). Perceptions of research from a second-year, multisite professional development school partnership. *The Journal of Educational Research, 95*, 75–83.

Goodlad, J. (1988). School-university partnerships for educational renewal: Rationale and concepts. In K. Sirotnik & J. Goodlad (Eds.), *School–university partnerships in action: Concepts, cases, and concerns* (pp. 3–31). New York, NY: McGraw-Hill.

Hmelo-Silver, C.E. (2004). Problem-based learning: What and how do students learn? *Educational Psychology Review, 16*, 235–265.

Holmes Group. (1986). *Tomorrow's teachers.* East Lansing, MI: Author.

King, M. B. (2002). Professional development to promote schoolwide inquiry. *Teaching and Teacher Education, 18*, 243–257.

Lemlech, J. K., Hertzog-Foliart, H., & Hackl, A. (2005). The Los Angeles professional practice school: A study of mutual impact. In L. Darling-Hammond (Ed.), *Professional development schools: Schools for developing the profession* (pp. 156–175). New York: Teachers College Press.

Lieberman, M.A., Yalom, I., & Miles, M. (1973). *Encounter groups: First facts.* New York: Free Press.

Linek, W. M., Fleener, C., Fazio, M., Raines, I. L., & Klakamp, K. (2003). The impact of shifting from 'how teachers teach' to 'how children learn.' *Journal of Educational Research, 97*(2), 78–89.

Marzano, R., Pickering, D., & Pollock, J. (2005). *Classroom instruction that works: Research based strategies for increasing student achievement.* Upper Saddle River, NJ: Pearson.

Mebane, D. J., & Galassi, J. P. (2003). Variables affecting collaborative research and leaning in a professional development school partnership. *The Journal of Educational Research, 96,* 259–268.

National Center for Education Statistics, (2005–2006). *Common Core Data.* Retrieved February 6, 2007, from http:www.nces.ed.gov/ccd/school

Pendergraft, E. M. (2007). *Teacher inquiry in a professional development school environment.* Unpublished doctoral dissertation Georgia State University. Available on the web at http://etd.gsu.edu/theses/available/etd-11202007-184211

Robinson, S. P., & Darling-Hammond, L. (2005). Change for collaboration, collaboration for change: Transforming teaching through school-university partnerships. In L. Darling-Hammond (Ed.), *Professional development schools: Schools for developing the profession* (pp. 203–220). New York: Teachers College Press.

Rogers, C. (2002). Defining reflection: Another look at John Dewey and reflective thinking. *Teachers College Record, 104,* 842–866.

Shaker, P. (2005). Growth: The consummate open-ended aspiration. In D. A. Breault & R. Breault (Eds.), *Experiencing Dewey: Insights for today's classrooms* (pp. 59–61). Indianapolis, IN: Kappa Delta Pi.

Silva, D.Y. (2000, April). *Mentor teachers ways of being and knowing in a professional development school.* Paper presented at the annual meeting of the American Educational Research Association, New Orleans, LA.

Slater, J. (1996) *Anatomy of a collaboration: Study of a college of education/public school partnership.* New York, NY: Routledge.

Smylie, M. A., Bay, M., & Tozer, S. E. (1999). Preparing teachers as agents of change. In Gary Griffin (Ed.), *The education of teachers, ninety-eighth yearbook of the National Society for the Study of Education* (pp. 29–62). Chicago: The University of Chicago Press.

Smyth, J. (1992). Teachers work and the politics of reflection. *American Educational Research Journal, 29,* 267–300.

Teitel, L. (1992). The impact of professional development school partnership on the preparation of teachers. *Teaching Education, 4,* 77–85.

Valli, L. (1993). Reconsidering technical and reflective concepts in teacher education. *Action in Teacher Education, 15*(2), 35–44.

Whitford, B. L. (2005). Permission, persistence, and resistance: Linking high school restructuring with teacher education reform. In L. Darling-Hammond (Ed.), *Professional development schools: Schools for developing the profession* (pp. 74–97). New York: Teachers College Press.

Zeichner, K., & Liston, D. (1996). *Reflective teaching: An introduction.* New Jersey: Lawrence Erlbaum Associates.

CHAPTER 7

AN APPROACH TO INCREASING STUDENT ACHIEVEMENT

Teacher-Intern-Professor Groups with Anchor Action Research

William L. Curlette and August Ogletree
Georgia State University

As our university entered into conversations with area schools systems regarding their possible involvement in implementing clinical teacher education within professional development schools, I (William Curlette) began discussions with the research directors of those school systems. From the beginning, the research directors expressed their desire that our professional development school (PDS) activities address, in some fashion, increasing student achievement. From a university perspective, we had also observed that state education officials and grant makers often asked about student achievement when considering whether to fund PDS activities. Furthermore, we all realized that across the country educational leaders in

Clinical Teacher Education, pages 117–127
Copyright © 2011 by Information Age Publishing
117

school systems and in colleges of education who are deciding whether or not to move toward a PDS model may ask for student achievement data. Such information helps to demonstrate the effectiveness of school-university partnerships and is beneficial for educators to consider as they contemplate whether to adopt a PDS approach.

We began our large scale implementation of a PDS network with accompanying research designed to compare student achievement at selected grade levels in our PDS's with results from matched comparison non-PDS sites. What we observed after a year of PDS activities was the resources that a university could devote to a school for increasing student achievement and for program evaluation were sometimes challenged in relation to the number of teachers and students in a school and their resource needs. For example, PDS interns at one school might be concentrated in primary grades, while a major focus of additional student achievement data at the elementary level beyond state-wide testing results for the overall project were collected on fourth-graders. Consequently, we began to realize that in the terminology of program evaluation, the *dosage* and *reach* of the PDS activities for student academic achievement in some situations may not be optimal for obtaining the desired results for the whole school within a year.

We believe that another reasonable unit to focus on for some of the academic achievement activities of a PDS would be a classroom rather than a whole school. In fact, a lot of qualitative research on the effectiveness of PDSs has been conducted in classrooms. To underscore the importance of examining the effectiveness of school-university partnerships at the classroom level and to underscore the classroom-based element of PDS relationships, we suggest that such activities be characterized and labeled as professional development schools and classrooms (PDSC). There are some PDS activities, such as a university faculty member working with a Parent Teacher Association or with school-wide professional development, that are legitimately delivered at the school level. Other activities, such as teaching-learning modules for student achievement, however, may initially be more appropriate at the classroom level. Emphasizing a classroom focus would also underscore the intense engagement of some classroom teachers who heartily participate in PDS collaborative approaches to clinical teacher education.

The realization that university and school resources are often specifically targeted at the classroom level and that investigations into student achievement needed to be similarly concentrated on the area of emphasis within a PDS collaborative led us to develop a classroom level approach for examining the effectiveness of our partnership work. We instituted the development of teaching-learning modules with a team consisting of classroom teacher(s), intern(s), and university professor(s). The team implements the modules and then employs a quantitative or mixed methods approach to assess student achievement. I (William Curlette) named this focused approach the Teacher-Intern-Professor (TIP) Model with Anchor Action Research (AAR). In this chapter, we (William Curlette and August Ogletree) will give an overview of the TIP model with AAR and then provide an example to illustrate its use. We will refer to our collaborative activities between a university and specific classrooms within a school as PDSC at some places in this chapter to introduce and support this new concept. We conclude the chapter by commenting on this approach and providing some future directions for the TIP model with AAR.

TEACHER-INTERN-PROFESSOR GROUPS WITH ANCHOR ACTION RESEARCH

According to the NCATE website (2010), "Professional development schools (PDSs) are innovative institutions formed through partnerships between professional education programs and P–12 schools. PDS partnerships have a four-fold mission: the preparation of new teachers, faculty development, inquiry directed at the improvement of practice, and enhanced student achievement." The TIP with AAR addresses all of these aspects of PDSs, including providing opportunities for higher education faculty to contribute to P–12 instruction. Although a TIP group might evaluate a teaching-learning module with a pretest and posttest in one classroom, AAR requires a comparison condition where the content is addressed in a traditional fashion and the same pre-post assessment is utilized. This comparison aids in reducing possible alternative explanations regarding gains in mean student achievement, if any, for the elementary, middle, or high school students taught by a module developed by the TIP group.

Teacher-Intern-Professor Model

The Teacher-Intern-Professor model was developed as a PDSC approach to support teaching interns' experiences while working to improve student achievement in the classroom. These interns are student teachers seeking to obtain a renewable teaching certificate through programs delivered at either an undergraduate or a master's degree level. The interns participate in TIP groups that have (a) a university faculty member to help design the research and (b) a classroom teacher to provide the setting and general support for the research effort. All participants in a TIP group can be involved in a literature search to support the selection and/or development of the content of the teaching-learning module and the classroom instructional activities that will be used. The university faculty member has content and/or pedagogical expertise in the subject area or grade level being taught. The intricacies of the content and expertise needed for the particular modules calls for coordination activities beyond the usual placement process. Thus, the formation of TIP groups calls for a logistical cooperation between the university in terms of selection of faculty to work in specific sites and the school system for placement of interns in particular PDSCs.

The TIP model also facilitates student achievement by providing additional specificity for the interns' teaching experiences. Teaching interns are given the opportunity to work both with their classroom teachers and university professors to help strengthen their teaching experiences and to explore up-to-date instructional methods that can be used with specific curricular topics. The interns and the classroom teachers can benefit through working with university faculty members to see how research projects related to teaching and learning are conducted. Within a TIP group, the professor may provide some just-in-time professional development for intern(s) and classroom teacher(s) on evaluation, research designs, and test score interpretations. The professor may also benefit by analyzing the effectiveness of teaching approaches in specific school-based contexts by obtaining additional opportunities for classroom research and by providing service to others in the area of education.

Anchor Action Research

A broad working definition of action research is offered by Hinchey (2008). Hinchey noted, "Action research is a process of systematic inquiry, usually cyclical, conducted by those inside a community rather than outside experts; its goal is to identify action that will generate improvements the researchers believe important" (p. 7). She indicated that the term action research has many variations often designated by a preceding word such as collaborative, which implies a group effort, or critical, which focuses on social issues such as unequal power arrangements.

The word we are prefacing action research with in order to define a particular approach is *anchor*. Anchor Action Research is concerned with changes in current policies and practices and includes three elements which allow researchers to anchor separate projects together into a potentially cohesive body of evidence. AAR projects are anchored (1) through commonalities among the studies in methodology, primarily quasi-experimental designs, and (2) through use of a general construct underlying the outcome measures (which for education is typically defined as student academic achievement outcome variables). There is a third anchor (3) which is that the projects attend to participants' inquiry skills and data interpretation abilities. Most AAR studies in education originate with the teacher and/or professor where the purpose of a study is to investigate changes in instructional practices. These three specifications focus the learning/teaching model on student outcomes and help to create an anchor, or commonality, across the research projects. The TIP group does have freedom to select the particular instructional practice(s) to be investigated and the content area for the instruction.

The AAR studies in our professional development schools network are all required to have a quantitative component where the achievement in comparison classrooms is used to help interpret the student achievement results in the TIP classrooms. In some situations, researchers may be able to randomize the placement of a TIP group between two or more classrooms. This could mean that over a series of TIP studies on the same topic, researchers could create a true experimental design. However, we realize that more likely the *participants* and the *duration* of the study are often not under the control of the teacher, intern, and professor involved in creating a TIP group. We have also found that our TIP participants are often interested in collecting additional qualitative information in addition to student academic achievement data. We believe that it is desirable that the research have a qualitative component to describe the contextual experiences of our TIP group; and thus, in these cases, the AAR study becomes a mixed methods design.

In the following paragraphs, we envision how AAR relates to other key ideas in action research which were previously mentioned. These ideas include (a) involvement of a community, (b) participants taking action, (c) improvements in teaching and learning, (d) systematic data collection, and (e) a cyclical process. The broader community in AAR studies is the partnership between the university and the school system, which is known traditionally as a PDS. Usually, the particular instance of a community would be a TIP group. The actions that are an outcome of our projects are improved teaching and at times the dissemination of a teaching-learning module.

By following the tenets and procedures of action research and quasi-experimental design, the AAR is systematic. However, the tradeoff for the structure offered by AAR is that, in comparison to action research, the researchers have less freedom to select a topic for their research and to choose the methodology. The advantage of the structure is that causal inference using quantitative data would tend to be improved and that a cycle of AAR studies would be conducted on the same general topic, which would aid in creating a body of research on that topic. Because AAR includes quasi-experimental design, a large body of literature exists that describes a number of possible research designs which can be used (see Shadish, Cook, & Campbell, 2002). AAR participants can employ a range of data analysis procedures, such as those discussed in statistical texts and articles, to analyze the data from a particular research design (e.g., see Rosenbaum, 2002 for observational studies).

In our experience, the first time a particular TIP group conducts a research study on an instructional method is usually the first time that that particular research team has worked together. Given a new team and a new research agenda, it is very likely that the first TIP study on a particular topic will be an exploratory study (see Tukey, 1977 for a discussion of exploratory research). The cyclical nature of action research would imply additional studies, and these additional studies are very likely to improve over time.

The notion of community in AAR becomes even more powerful when it is expanded from a single TIP group to a much larger TIP group or collection of TIP groups (for community of researchers, see Herr & Anderson, 2005; Hendricks, 2009). Hinchey (2008) supports the notion of creating a community of researchers. She emphasizes:

> Many action researchers consider having a research community indispensible, even though (as noted earlier) many models don't consider or promote them as a necessary part of the work. Communities provide researchers with opportunities for discussions with like-minded others who share both an interest in inquiry and a passion to make things better. (p. 119)

To illustrate how a TIP group might design a project that could extend across multiple classrooms, we now turn to a specific example of a TIP project conducted as an AAR study in two mathematics classrooms in our professional development schools network. The community of professionals involved in this study included one professor, two teachers, and two interns who worked together to design and implement a unit of instruction. This TIP group in our urban network demonstrates the kinds of focused research that can lead to improved clinical teacher education and improved student performance.

A TIP GROUP CONDUCTS AN AAR STUDY ON STUDENT ACHIEVEMENT IN AN ELEMENTARY MATHEMATICS CLASSROOM

The members of this TIP group designed an AAR study for two fourth-grade classrooms where the teaching-learning module was a six week unit on geometry. These TIP classrooms were in a PDS elementary school with over 90% of the students eligible for free or reduced price meals. The school, located in an urban school system, was a Title I school that had not met its Adequate Yearly Progress (AYP) goals for the previous school year. The school was part of our PDS network and a beneficial relationship developed among several teachers, student interns, and the university liaison who was assigned to the school.

Two early childhood education student interns participated in the TIP group while they were completing their student teaching internships. A requirement of the internships was that the interns work in their classrooms five days a week for the second half of their internships. These interns were in the same classrooms for an extended period of time, which facilitated the TIP group with AAR. The interns met every two weeks with their teachers and with a research professor during the creation of the unit of instruction and then as the unit was taught to the students.

Two classroom teachers both taught fourth grade at the same PDS site. They had been teaching in this school for several years and had supported student interns in their classrooms during prior years. Consequently, they were familiar with the procedures and activities which accompanied hosting a student intern. One teacher taught in a general education class and had been teaching for over twenty years in this same urban school system. The other teacher taught in an intervention classroom, and she had been teaching for three years in this urban school system. Students in the intervention classroom typically scored below grade level in reading and language arts on the third-grade statewide end-of-year achievement test.

The university professor in the TIP group had previously worked as a university liaison in the PDS program. She had an elementary mathematics background and taught mathematics methods courses to undergraduate early childhood preparation students at the university. This professor had experience working with faculty in the school for several years prior to the TIP project. These years of experience had allowed her to develop a relationship with the administration, faculty, and staff within the school. The professor did not serve as the supervisor to the student interns but as the university liaison for this PDS site where she worked with teachers and interns at the school one day a week.

The TIP group curriculum for the geometry unit as well as the comparison group curriculum for the same topic followed the relatively new statewide integrated mathematics curriculum. However, the TIP groups had a university professor to help explain and implement the standards during the study. In addition, the classes had access to manipulatives for teaching, which were purchased from funds provided by a small mini-grant. To understand student achievement, we relied on teacher-made tests used for both groups. We utilized teacher-made mathematics tests because we felt teacher-made tests have more content validity for a particular unit of instruction than a standardized achievement test.

The primary focus of the research investigation included the following question: Are there significant differences in mean student achievement posttest scores on geometry between the fourth-grade TIP classrooms and comparison classrooms using teacher-made tests? The pretest on geometry was given at the beginning of the 6-week unit, and a different posttest on geometry was given at the end of the unit. The scores on the tests were the percentage correct scores and could range from 0% correct to 100% correct. A practical constraint was that the classroom teachers insisted on giving a different pretest and posttest. The comparison group classrooms were similar to the TIP classrooms and consisted of one general education classroom and one intervention classroom at fourth grade within the same school as the TIP groups.

Out of the 71 students in the TIP classrooms and comparison classrooms, we had both pretest and posttest scores for 64 of the children. We wanted to provide some control for ability in geometry that the TIP group students and comparison group students may have had at the beginning of the study, so we created four blocks of scores based on the pretest scores of the 64 students. Using a two-way factorial ANOVA with four blocks on the pretest for one factor, a two level treatment factor (TIP groups versus comparison groups), and the posttest geometry scores as the dependent variable, the results indicated that the TIP group geometry curriculum benefitted the lowest two groups on the geometry pretest.

To follow-up on the ANOVA and to explore the data as an aid in designing future studies, we collapsed the lowest two groups on the pretest (labeled block one, which was the overall low group on geometry pretest scores) and the highest two groups on the pretest (labeled block two, which was the overall high group on geometry pretest scores). For block one ($n_{TIP} = 24$, $n_{CS} = 11$), we compared the geometry posttest mean of the TIP groups (79.1%) with the posttest geometry mean of the comparison groups (57.1%), using an independent t-test. The t-test indicated that the means were statistically significantly different ($t = 3.9$, $df = 33$, $p < .001$). Using block two ($n_{TIP} = 11$, $n_{CS} = 18$), we compared the geometry posttest mean of the TIP groups (91.8%) with the posttest geometry mean of the comparison groups (86.3%), by employing an independent t-test. The t-test indicated that the means were not statistically significantly different ($t = 1.8$, $df = 27$, $p = .077$). As shown in Figure 7.1, the mean difference on the geometry posttest between the TIP and comparison groups is much greater for the lower ability students as measured by the pretest (block one) than the higher ability students (block two).

To help interpret these results, mean difference effect sizes were computed using pooled standard deviations. In other words, a mean of the comparison group is subtracted from a mean of the TIP group and the difference is divided by the pooled standard deviation for the two groups. For block one, the pretest effect size was .16 in favor of the TIP group and the posttest effect size was 1.42 in favor of the TIP group. Cohen (1987) suggests as a guideline that a standardized mean difference effect size of .8 be considered large. Therefore, the effect size for block one on the post-

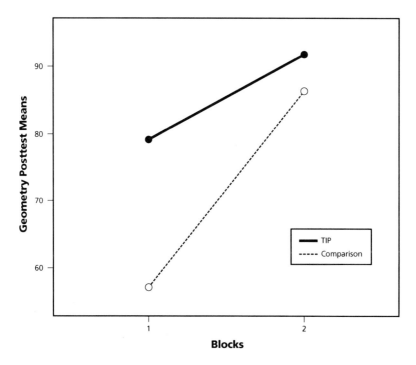

Figure 7.1   Geometry posttest means for blocks one and two by TIP and comparison groups.

test (1.42), even in comparison to the initial effect size which favored the TIP group (.16), is very large. For block two, the effect size for the pretest was .48 in favor of the TIP group and the effect size for the posttest was .70 in the direction that supports the TIP group. So the TIP group started out ahead of the comparison group with an effect size of .48 and ended up a little more ahead of the comparison group with the .70 effect size; however, the *t*-test comparing the means did not reach statistical significance with alpha equal to .05. In conclusion, these results provide initial support for the success of the TIP group and sufficient evidence to merit replication of this TIP group teaching-learning module.

SUMMARY: CLINICAL TEACHER EDUCATION USING TIP GROUPS AND AN AAR APPROACH

As we have discussed in this chapter, we believe a Teacher-Intern-Professor (TIP) group using an Anchor Action Research (AAR) approach fits well within a clinical model for teacher education. Preliminary data from a TIP group using an AAR model supports the idea that if clinical teacher education is to impact student achievement, a focused content areas, small scale studies may yield more beneficial results than large scale analyses of achievement in an urban PDS network. From a research perspective, such an approach contributes a real world example of an increase in academic student achievement within professional development schools. The TIP with AAR approach links research design with classroom-based instruction in ways that are practical and worthwhile. Teachers and interns can see that their work has made a difference in students' learning and school administrators and researchers are pleased to have data to support the impact of their collaboration. In fact, after listening to a conference presentation of the results from the TIP study shared in this chapter, a high level administrator from the school system where the TIP study was implemented, was so enthusiastic about the results he said, "You have hit a home-run."

In closing, if the TIP classroom research is viewed as part of a professional development school relationship and a PDS relationship brings additional resources from the synergist effect of the partnership, then the TIP group results support the PDS clinical teacher education partnership. In such a way, this approach has potential for making important contributions to both teacher education and P–12 education. By using a TIP group implementation of Anchor Action Research studies, we can accumulate increasing evidence of the effectiveness of Professional Development Schools and Classrooms (PDSC) on increasing student achievement. Also, we believe that additional research could examine the effect of TIP groups for increasing the research ability and test score interpretation ability for all members of a TIP group. In the future, to improve the generalizability of the results of TIP with AAR studies and to increase sample size (due to the TIP studies typically having only a limited number of classrooms involved), a meta-analysis approach to summarizing research should also be entertained. In addition to the research contributions of such studies, the importance of the curricular innovations contributed by the TIP groups should not be overlooked. As teaching-learning modules are developed and validated for increasing student achievement in conjunction with other desirable educational outcomes, avenues for disseminating the materials to interns, teachers, and professors should also be explored in order to share these units and pedagogical approaches with other practitioners. In this way, as the Anchor Action Research findings help to validate the importance of school-university partnerships, the Teacher-Intern-Professor group's contribution to both research and practice can also be increasingly recognized and valued.

REFERENCES

Cohen, J. (1987). *Statistical power analysis for the behavioral sciences* (Rev. ed.). Hillsdale, NJ: Lawrence Erlbaum Associates.

Hendricks, C. (2009). *Improving schools through action research: A comprehensive guide for educators* (2nd ed.). Upper Saddle River, NJ: Pearson.

Herr, K., & Anderson, G. (2005). *The action research dissertation: A guide for students and faculty.* Thousand Oaks, CA: Sage.

Hinchey, P. H. (2008). *Action research.* New York, NY: Peter Lang.

NCATE (2010). *Welcome to the professional development schools website.* Retrieved from http://www.ncate.org/ProfessionalDevelopmentSchools/tabid/497/Default.aspx

Rosenbaum, P. R. (2002). *Observational studies* (2nd ed.). New York: Springer-Verlag.

Shadish, W., Cook, T., & Campbell, D. (2002). *Experimental and quasi-experimental designs for generalized causal inference.* Boston, MA: Houghton Mifflin Company.

Tukey, J. (1977). *Exploratory data analysis.* Reading, MA: Addison-Wesley.

CHAPTER 8

MAKING A DIFFERENCE IN TEACHER DEVELOPMENT AND HIGH QUALITY TEACHING

Joseph R. Feinberg, Brian Williams, Dee Taylor
Georgia State University

Kezia McNeal Curry
University of Hawaii at Manoa

Lou Matthews
Department of Education, Bermuda

Lin Black
Georgia State University

Unlike ever before, the challenge of equipping today's public educators with professional development opportunities that can be coupled with job-embedded skills is imperative. Educators prefer to engage in professional learning that positively impacts teacher preparation, decreases teacher attrition, and above all, increases PK–12 student achievement. That is, educators want a variety of effective models that provide intentional results as the

Clinical Teacher Education, pages 129–146
Copyright © 2011 by Information Age Publishing
129

outcome. The *Professional Development Schools Network* (PDSN) partnerships afforded university-school professional learning experiences that were relevant, ongoing, sustained, and job-embedded. PDSN offered many venues for the university to collaborate with the teachers and leaders from our fifteen professional development schools and partnering school districts.

There is a wide-spread consensus that professional development is one of the most needed aspects in education today; however, much of the learning in professional development is regarded as ineffective (Guskey, 1997). Too often educators note that the learning in which they engage is not well-planned, not supported, does not respect their time, appears faddish and meaningless, and is not research or evidence-based. The training may be valuable, but frequently it cannot be implemented in classrooms because of inadequate resources or structural support (Guskey, 1992). There are, indeed, successful professional development models that research shows have become widely accepted as valid and effective means of professional growth. Our professional development schools partnership tapped several variations of these models in order to lead to richer partnerships, deeper learning for professionals, and results that benefited the PK–12 teachers, the university teacher-preparation faculty and the classroom students. These models included, but were not limited to the following: 1) training, 2) observation/assessment, 3) involvement in a development and improvement process, 4) study groups, 5) inquiry/action research, 6) individually guided activities, 7) mentoring, and 8) professional learning communities (Drago-Severson, 1994; Morrissey, 2000; Sparks & Loucks-Horsley, 1989).

Professional development initiatives in our urban collaborative network required an understanding of both public school teachers' needs and interests and an ability to be aware of and capitalize on university resources and expertise. I, Dee Taylor, served as one of the first *boundary spanners* for PDSN, and in my role I was able to make connections across these two contexts. I retired as professional development Executive Director from one of our urban partner districts to serve as the first PDSN Project Director at the university. Leading a large metropolitan district's professional learning initiatives and knowing that the aforementioned development challenges were real, I arrived at the university prepared and motivated to help build bridges. We began with valuing each others' arenas and skills; planning collaboratively; implementing, evaluating, research; and exploring innovative and sound professional learning experiences with our partner school districts and schools. PDS², a Teacher Quality Enhancement grant awarding $6.1 million, provided a variety of funding venues to assist with professional learning implementation (see models above). In this chapter, we detail a few of our stories illustrating well-planned, effectively executed and sustained training.

LIN BLACK'S JOURNEY WITH CROSS CAREER LEARNING COMMUNITIES

Leaving retirement to return to the life of helping and retaining teachers gave me such energy! I, Lin Black, accepted the position and the challenge offered at the university to team with the National Commission on Teaching and America's Future (NCTAF) to provide support to newly-graduated educators as well as mentor teachers in a highly-developed professional learning community called a Cross Career Learning Community (CCLC).

The project partners, in addition to the university and NCTAF, included the state board of regents systems, the state systemic teacher education program, and 12 schools from four metropolitan area school systems. Evaluation results indicated that the CCLCS were effective at retaining teachers while enhancing their teaching skills. By the third year, additional schools and systems recognized the value of the project and asked to join the training.

Our project was designed around the state's framework for accomplished teaching, now adopted as the state's definition of quality teaching by the state's Professional Standards Commission, the state's Department of Education, and the state's Board of Regents system. The state framework for accomplished teaching as well as its enlarged version, the state's extended framework for teaching, defined the knowledge, skills, and other attributes of accomplished teaching in six areas: 1) content and curriculum, 2) knowledge of students, 3) classroom environments, 4) assessment, 5) planning and instruction, and 6) professionalism. The framework was first introduced to teacher candidates during their preparation program. It can be used by experienced teachers and faculty to observe and support beginning teachers and by all teachers to self-assess and develop their growth as professionals.

Establishing unique professional learning communities was at the core of this induction project. These Cross Career Learning Communities offered a safe place for members to gather and support each other as they worked through their dilemmas and needs. The CCLC was comprised of trained facilitators, university interns and beginning teachers, mentor teachers, and university faculty members in various combinations. The groups were encouraged to meet at least once a month or more often if possible to build a supportive "family" unit as they worked together. The educators trained to become CCLC facilitators took part in a week-long institute where they were taught how to use the three project components and how to set up a learning community once they returned to their schools. Essentially, the learning communities, or CCLCs, were trained to use the following three components that were brought together or developed as part of this project to carry out the work of the community. These are still in operation in our PDSN's today: *Critical Friends Groups (CFG) Protocols; The BRIDGE* (Building Resources: Induction and development for state educators), a peer-reviewed and interactive online resource and mentoring site for teachers (synchronous and asynchronous); and finally, *Professional Growth Plan: An Observation And Self-Assessment Tool.*

The four major goals of the project that the evaluators examined at the conclusion of the grant were as follows:

1. *Create learning communities and improve teacher satisfaction in high-needs schools.* My team and I coordinated the training of Cross Career Learning Communities (CCLCs) in order to support and retain new university graduates as well as all experienced teachers in high-need schools (five cohorts of about 30 teachers each; these 150 trained teachers were called facilitators). During the course of the grant, the facilitators formed approximately 50 CCLCs. They expressed high satisfaction at both the beginning and the end of each school year.
2. *Increase retention rate of teachers in high-need schools, especially of new teachers.* Our retention rate of new teachers returning to their schools began at 63% during the first year of the grant before any intervention was carried out. Once the new teachers participated in CCLCs, the retention rate rose to 86% during the second year, and measured 93% at the completion of the project.
3. *Improve quality of teacher skills in high-need schools.* When we examined teachers' skills, their portfolios showed increases in depth and in scope in each domain of the state's framework for accomplished teaching in content and curriculum, knowledge of students, learning environments, assessment, planning and instruction, and professionalism. Teachers' instructional plans and materials exemplified data-driven monitoring practices. Evaluation results showed a variety of assessments to instruct, remediate, and enrich students through refined and focused teaching practices as well as appropriate instructional strategies.
4. *Increase PK–12 student achievement and school performance in high-needs schools.* In comparing the elementary comparison and treatment schools, we noted relevant results. Examining only the current year, passing rates could conceal some progress made in the project. For example, the second year results showed that the treatment elementary school pass rate was lower than the pass rate for the comparison schools. However, in the final year's data, the treatment schools' pass rate was higher than the comparison schools pass rate in five of the 21 tests: third-grade science, fourth-grade science, fourth-grade social studies, fifth-grade math, and fifth-grade science. This difference, higher pass rates in five of the 21 tests as opposed to 0 of the 21 tests, was statistically significant ($z = 2.38$, $p < .009$). In middle schools, the passing rates for treatment schools were higher than the passing rates in comparison schools for 13 of the 13 tests reported.

The same pattern continued from the previous year. In high schools, the passing rates were higher for treatment schools for two of the five graduation tests and were also higher in two of the seven end-of-course tests. This contrasted with the previous year results where the treatment school passing rates were lower for each of the high school graduation tests and lower in seven out of eight end-of-course tests; however the increase for the current year was not statistically significant ($z = 1.508$, $p = .066$).

Our evaluation report showed that the CCLCs were perceived as beneficial in contributing to a supportive work environment that enhanced professional growth, collegiality and motivation to remain in the teaching profession.

DR. BRIAN WILLIAMS' ELEMENTARY SCHOOL ENDEAVOR

I, Brian Williams, an assistant professor of early childhood education at the university, have been involved with the Professional Development School Network (PDSN) from the second year of the grant. I have served as a university liaison at Springdale Elementary School (pseudonym) for the past three years. Springdale served approximately 350 students in grades pre-K through five. Ninety-nine percent of the students were African American. The remaining 1% of the students were categorized as multiracial. In terms of socio-economic status, 89% percent of the students received free and reduced lunch (2007–2008 Report Card). The school was recognized at both the district and state level for effectiveness and performance on measures of educational accountability.

As the PDSN liaison, I was responsible for supporting the relationship and interactions between the university and Springdale. This included supervising the placement of pre-service teacher interns, participating in the building of school-community partnerships, leveraging the resources of PDSN to meet the needs of school and/or university, and providing guidance and expertise regarding specific issues faced by the school and/or university. More specifically, I spent the majority of this time supporting the school's objectives regarding science and mathematics education reform.

The latest standards for school mathematics, as seen in the release of the state's performance standards, called for dynamic shifts in mathematics teaching. These shifts required teachers to move away from teacher-centered, traditional approaches, which viewed mathematics as a static set of isolated facts and procedures, towards a view of mathematics as dynamic, related ideas. Teachers were expected to create classrooms where students engaged in challenging mathematics tasks, utilized a variety of approaches, and communicated their ideas (NCTM, 2000).

Another important part of the vision for the state's performance standards was that success in mathematics need not be limited to a few select students, but that *all* students experience greater success in school mathematics. Thus, all students can learn mathematics with success through teaching excellence and support. Helping all students to be successful in mathematics has been an especially daunting task in urban school districts across the nation. For example, according to the latest national "report card" on the progress of the nation's urban districts in mathematics, persistent achievement disparities remain between urban districts and the rest of the nation (with the exception of Austin and Charlotte) in both grades four and eight (Lutkus & Weiner, 2003; National Center for Education Statistics, 2006). Additionally, racial achievement gaps throughout the nation's districts are persistent and pervasive.

During the first year of my tenure at an elementary school in the metropolitan area, I was approached by school administrators about the school's desire to improve mathematics instruction at the school. I utilized PDSN resources to facilitate a PK–5 Mathematics Endorsement program aimed at enhancing the content and pedagogical knowledge of mathematics teachers in the elementary grades. Lou Matthews, then an assistant professor of mathematics education at the university, was recruited to design and implement the course. Lou's experience and extensive knowledge base regarding mathematics education, specifically in urban schools, made him well-suited for the task. His involvement also supported the program's use of equity pedagogy, also called culturally relevant pedagogy, and significantly enhanced the likelihood of success for the predominantly African American student population enrolled in the school.

The purpose of this facet of the Springdale-GSU PDSN relationship was to transform the ways that Springdale teachers thought about and taught mathematics. Fostering a professional environment where teachers could reflect on practice, collaborate with each other, and share experiences with colleagues across grade levels sustained this transformation. To realize this purpose, we designed a school reform agenda around three priorities: 1) building capacity within the school by encouraging teachers to serve as intellectual leaders in mathematics, 2) thinking and acting "outside the box" in school leadership, and 3) collective learning in action through Cross Career Learning Communities (CCLC) and Lesson Study.

The PK–5 Mathematics Endorsement was designed to cultivate the mathematics content and pedagogical content knowledge of in-service teachers. In addition to these topics, the endorsement also focused on the development of conceptual understanding in mathematics as well as the utilization of the best practices in the classroom. The endorsement was delivered as a series of four graduate-level courses. Each course met for a total of 50 hours. The sequence for the course content was: Understanding Numbers and Operations (Spring 2007), Understanding Algebra (Summer 2007),

Understanding Geometry (Fall 2007), and Understanding Data Analysis and Probability (Spring 2008). There was a ten-hour field experience requirement in the last course. For the courses that met during the spring and fall semesters, the participants met once a week for 12 weeks. Each course session lasted for four hours and ten minutes. During the one summer session, participants met daily for five hours over a two-week period (ten work days). Participants in the endorsement were drawn from elementary schools across a metropolitan school district. Six teachers successfully completed the mathematics endorsement course series. All six of these teachers were employed at an elementary school within the school district.

The main goal of the mathematics endorsement was to enhance the teachers' understanding of the content so that they might engage their students with challenging mathematics ideas. This goal required that teachers have a sound understanding of (a) the content, (b) the ideas that underpin the ways that *their* children understand mathematics, and (c) the nature of mathematics and mathematical knowledge. In order to accomplish this goal, Lou organized the mathematics endorsement around two important ideas: *culturally relevant teaching* and *cognitively demanding tasks*.

Culturally Relevant Teaching in Mathematics

A growing number of researchers have addressed equity and achievement concerns by articulating the potential of culturally relevant teaching perspectives to improve the mathematics achievement and teaching of students in urban districts. Educators have articulated connections between culturally relevant teaching and national standards for teaching mathematics (Enyedy, Mukhopadhyay, & Danish, 2006; Gutstein, Lipman, Hernandez, & de los Reyes, 1997; Leonard & Guha, 2002; Matthews, 2003; Nelson-Barber & Estrin, 1995; Tate, 2004). As Ladson-Billings (1994, 1995a, 1995b, 1997) highlighted, the purpose of culturally relevant teaching is to frame teaching more broadly in ways that help students to achieve academically, socially, politically and culturally. Mathematics tasks that are culturally relevant 1) explicitly require students to inquire about themselves, their communities, and the world about them; 2) draw from connections to other subjects and issues; 3) are mathematically rich and cognitively demanding; 4) are real-world focused, requiring students to make sense of the world through mathematics; and 5) help students make empowered decisions about themselves, communities and world.

Throughout the endorsement, mathematics was presented as a cultural subject. For example, when discussing data analysis and probability, the teachers investigated how data was used in the school and the larger community. Similarly, the course sessions on algebra explored the connections between algebra and the use of patterns in the community. The geometry course incorporated examples of space and shapes as they existed in the school and community. In every course, teachers searched for connections between the content and the lives of their children.

Cognitively Demanding Tasks

Current reform efforts in mathematics require teachers to be able to identify, create and even transform traditional mathematics tasks in order to engage students' thinking. These tasks should emphasize the learning of rich mathematics concepts, multiple representations and strategies, and the communication of one's reasoning when problem solving (NCTM, 2000). Stein, Smith, Henningsen and Silver (2000) suggest that tasks with which mathematics lessons are framed are the "basis of opportunities" for learning mathematics (p. 11). In addition to focusing on covering a full spectrum of mathematical content, the National Assessment of Education Progress (NAEP) emphasizes cognitive demand as an essential component of mathematical tasks.

Stein et al. (2000) classify two types of higher level cognitively demanding tasks: *Procedures with Connections to Understanding, Meaning and Concepts*, and *Doing Mathematics: Procedures with Connection* tasks require students to use procedures in ways that build conceptual understanding of important concepts. The second category, *Doing Mathematics*, is often non-algorithmic, unpredictable, and requires multiple ways of representing concepts. Open-ended word problems which might involve a series of steps and representations including symbolism, graphs and verbal explanations often fall in this category. The emphasis on *doing* as the key endeavor in learning mathematics is easily seen in national benchmarks about science teaching and learning.

In order to truly incorporate an understanding of cognitively demanding tasks into their pedagogy, the teachers enrolled in the endorsement participated in discussions around three essential questions: what is good mathematics teaching? what is mathematics? and who can learn it? These questions created opportunities for the teachers to reflect on their ideas regarding mathematics and mathematics teaching.

In an effort to challenge the teachers' ideas regarding mathematics and mathematics teaching, Lou employed two strategies during the endorsement. First, he integrated the mathematics content being presented during the endorsement with pedagogy experiences and demonstrations of cognitively demanding tasks. By modeling the use of cognitively demanding tasks in the endorsement sessions, he presented the teachers with the opportunity (a) to develop their own understanding of the content and (b) to reassess the plausibility of using these tasks in their own teaching.

Second, Lou led the participants in vision building around mathematics teaching and learning. Vision building is a process used as a means of building consensus among the members of a community. Members of the community worked together to develop a vision of their collective future. In the mathematics endorsement, Lou used vision building to aid the teachers in creating a vision of effective mathematics teaching and learning. The resulting vision included ideas such as cognitively demanding tasks and student-centered instruction. Furthermore, by participating in vision building, the teachers developed a body of valued community knowledge which assumed the need for cultural relevance and higher level task in mathematics instruction and learning.

As a result of the relationships among university faculty, the faculty of Springdale Elementary School developed a strong educational community focused on the effective teaching and learning of mathematics. Furthermore, the endorsement course prepared the teachers to engage their students in mathematics that was rooted in the students' cultural norms and lived experiences. Although the endorsement course has ended, the faculty members at Springdale remained committed to continuing to develop their understanding of effective science and mathematics instruction. The partnership with the university has been an integral part of this work.

KEZIA MCNEAL CURRY'S JOURNEY IN A PDSN MIDDLE SCHOOL

I, Kezia McNeal Curry, an assistant professor of middle childhood education at the university, was involved with the PDSN project from the first year of the grant and continued my involvement in subsequent years at the same middle school. This PDS school had an enrollment of over 1,300 students. Fifty-seven percent were Hispanic, 23% African American, 12% Asian, and 6% white. Eighty-four percent of the students received free and reduced lunch. As it so happened, the middle school was in the same community in which I lived, which gave me an even more vested interest in the success of the members of the school community.

During the third year of the project, I conducted a professional learning course available for all teachers in the school. The primary objective of the five week course, Culturally Relevant Interdisciplinary Instructional Strategies (CRIIS), was to convene teachers from across the disciplines and introduce them to and support their implementation of the principles of culturally responsive pedagogy (Irvine & Armento, 2001) and the five dimensions of multicultural education (Banks & Banks, 2004).

I provided teachers with immediate and ongoing opportunities to use the knowledge in meaningful ways in their classrooms. The content areas of the teachers varied and included individuals from language arts, band, math, science, social studies, family and consumer sciences, health, and school counseling. Using the data from the middle school's plan for school improvement, the county- and state-developed curriculum standards, and from professional expertise, I developed a course on using CRIIS. Some of the key strategies of CRIIS included using concepts or knowledge from a different content area to relate to a concept in the main content area, grouping students heterogeneously, using students' languages and language patterns to teach content concepts, drawing upon local happenings and concerns for content area lessons, and providing creative opportunities for students to express their understanding of subject matter.

On the first evening of the course, I asked the teachers to write their own definitions of *multicultural education*. The most common terms used were words such as *diverse, equal, culture, different, teaching*, and *learning*. Overall, the teachers defined *multicultural education* as a way to make sure that all students were given the best tools possible to learn regardless of their various backgrounds. From that foundation, I built on the teachers' actual multicultural educational experiences by leading them through three primary exercises along with several secondary exercises. The successful completion of the exercises was predicated upon the teachers' inclusion of students' diverse backgrounds and high academic content. The first exercise was based on a news article about a middle school's effort to change the school cafeteria offerings to include more healthy options. I grouped teachers across disciplines and asked them to develop learning activities relative to the article's content for each of the eight content areas identified by their county handbook (e.g., language arts, math, social studies, science, physical education, technology, character, and fine arts). The second exercise also required the teachers to be grouped heterogeneously. I provided them several documents from a local bank, and their task was to develop a learning activity that would support a key concept from their individual content areas. The third exercise pertained to diverse perspectives. The teachers were assigned different roles, and I read a story to them. At the end of the story, I asked questions that had to be answered based on their assigned roles. Since the teachers were not aware of the different roles at first, a critical component of the exercise was helping them to identify how perspective influences understanding.

As culminating exercises, the teachers completed two major projects: a classroom profile and a mini-action research project in which they used feedback gathered from the classroom profile to develop an approach to integrate CRIIS. The classroom profile had two parts: 1) complete a classroom profile for two of your classes that identifies several unique categories of characteristics of your students based on culture and/or academic interests, providing charts and graphs for the profile, and 2) develop a question about your teaching context from your classroom profile. The mini-action research project was based on the teachers' questions developed from the classroom profile. The questions were presented in a more formal way along with details that outlined a specific plan of action, results of the plan implementation, potential directions for future investigation of the question, and personal and professional reaction to the plan implementation.

Inspection of the teachers' classroom profiles showed what kinds of connections teachers thought may have existed between students' academic performance and their culture. The instructions for the classroom profile were intentionally broad, so that the teachers could explore questions that were important to them. From the profiles, the teachers made connections between students' choice of band instrument and classroom behavior, students' religion and participation in certain class discussions, students' language proficiency and math learning, students' home interactions and academic productivity, and other connections. One specific example of a connection was the health teacher's deeper inquiry about the students' ethnic culture and their description of a typical nutritious meal. The United States Department of Agriculture (USDA) highlights the use of the Food Pyramid to encourage healthy consumption. As a result of the classroom profile, the health teacher recognized that in order to maximize students' understanding of eating healthy, their cultural context had to be considered. The classroom profiles gave teachers the opportunity to identify and test their assumptions about students' academic performance and teachers' effectiveness in delivering instruction.

The teachers' action research plans indicated that all five dimensions of multicultural education were implemented. Content integration and equity pedagogy were used most often, while prejudice reduction, knowledge construction, and empowering school culture and social structure were used occasionally. The key questions for each teacher centered on how a deeper understanding of relevant aspects of their students' cultures might enhance instruction in a particular content area. An example of an action research plan was the bilingual focus of a math teacher. Her math class consisted of only Hispanic and African American students who needed additional help in math. From her classroom profile, her attention was drawn to her students' language use. Her plan included pairing Hispanic students with African American students on a series of particular assignments in which each student had to provide an explanation of the work using English and Spanish. This activity reinforced the students' math comprehension skills as well as their language skills.

The action research projects were successful on several levels. First, the teachers were afforded the opportunity to specifically reflect on their instruction, particularly in relation to the significant role of culture. Second, the teachers gained practice in developing and implementing culturally relevant content area instruction, even though not every strategy and/or activity the teacher used was shown to be effective or appropriate for the situations. Through this process the teachers were able to refine some of their practices. Third, the teachers were able to collaborate in ways that promoted the positive development of their middle-school students. Although the school did engage in a number of practices that define middle-level education, such as team structure, adapted counseling practices, and integrated academic enrichment, the teachers still struggled with maintaining the integrity of such practices while also being responsible for traditional expectations associated with high stakes testing and meeting adequate yearly progress under *No Child Left Behind*. Additionally, some of the teachers were novice educators and grappled with all of the issues associated with being new. Finally, the teachers expressed that they felt successful in carrying out their action research and indicated that they were interested in furthering their understanding and practice.

As part of a larger investigation, I expanded the course objectives beyond the five-week period. I invited teachers to explore their action research questions through conversations and classroom observations. As a result of the professional learning course, my relationship with the teachers became more solidified. Even when not specifically engaged in the formal research activities, the conversations often involved ways to continually enhance professional learning about culture and academic achievement. The opportunity for this kind of professional growth that brought about tangible positive results was made possible through the strong PDSN partnership.

JOSEPH R. FEINBERG MAKES A DIFFERENCE IN TEACHER DEVELOPMENT AND HIGH QUALITY TEACHING IN A PDSN HIGH SCHOOL

I, Joseph R. Feinberg, joined the PDS project during the second year of the grant when I was an assistant professor of social studies education at the university. My work as a PDSN university liaison at Gilbert High School (pseudonym) provided many opportunities for collaboration and mutual renewal. Gilbert High School (GHS) had an enrollment of over 2,300 diverse students with 30% African American, 14% Asian, 47% Hispanic, 7% Caucasian, and 2% multiracial (2007–2008 Report Card). In addition, GHS was a Title I school with 71% of the students eligible for free/reduced meals and 24% with limited English proficiency.

As a PDS university liaison, the majority of my weekly time at GHS was spent visiting, meeting, or informally conversing with teachers, administrators, and student teachers or interns. Through such interaction, I established a positive rapport with many of the teachers, administrators and the PDS site coordinator. The positive rapport with GHS faculty afforded an environment where contacts from the school were comfortable collaborating through the PDSN network. For example, some teachers and administrators approached me when they thought university resources or my expertise would be helpful. The most frequent use of my expertise was through student teachers or interns. With the cooperation and support of school administrators, including the PDSN site-based coordinator and teachers, I organized meetings, workshops, and communication among student teachers/interns and their mentors or partnership teachers. In addition, I assisted university colleagues with student teacher placements, mentor concerns and problems, or advice about the school demographics or climate for research. However, I was concerned that the positive success through student teachers and interns was not sufficient to transform the relationship into a viable long-term PDSN (Teitel, 2003).

The PDS^2 (a federal TQE grant) provided funding and therefore substantive opportunities for professional development, but a limited amount of the grant money was spent at GHS on professional development during the first two years of the grant. The PDS^2 grant supplied each network school an iBook computer and a video camera (among other technology). Fortunately, Tim Merritt, who was a technology expert at the university, was partially funded through the PDSN initiative to provide iBook computer and video camera training for partnership teachers and interns. The technology training facilitated by Tim was well attended, and his training afforded an essential model for in-service and pre-service teacher professional development that was possible through the PDS network. Such professional development was previously proposed and integrated in the PDSN goals and school improvement plan, but never quite realized. In other words, the PDSN goals established at GHS were comprehensive, yet never fully satisfied. "Full-fledged PDSNs have comprehensive goals," argued Teitel (2003), which "go beyond the student teacher component to address the professional development needs of in-service faculty" (p. 75).

The success of the technology in-service training and continued effort to build bridges between the high school and university provided a foundation for additional collaboration. Teitel (2003) notes that "higher levels of joint planning and collaborative decision making lead to greater interdependence" (p. 75). Through my role as the PDSN university liaison, I bridged the expertise of university faculty with the expressed needs of the high school. As a result of such collaboration, I coordinated the participation of nine university faculty members participating in over 20 sessions for two professional development conferences and three grant writing workshops.

The professional development conferences at GHS were spearheaded by an assistant principal who learned about the PDSN goals and PDS^2 grant funding through the school site coordinator. The assistant principal approached me and requested PDS^2 grant support and university faculty presentations for the spring GHS professional development conference. I was thrilled that my previous networking activities succeeded in providing this wonderful opportunity to satisfy PDS goals and build a stronger bridge between the two institutions. The invitation for the university to participate in the GHS Professional Learning Conference was immediately accepted, and I quickly sent an email announcement that solicited presentation proposals from my colleagues at the university.

Within a week, five university faculty members from diverse content areas, such as language and literacy, technology, and special education, responded with presentation proposals. The assistant principal was very pleased with the proposals and accepted all five after careful review, but she also desired math and science presentations. As a result, I individually met with colleagues in math and science education, and two agreed to participate. Half of the Professional Learning Conference sessions were facilitated by seven PDSN/GSU faculty members and the other sessions were presented by GHS teachers and administrators.

Positive Feedback

Conference evaluations from teachers and administrators were overwhelmingly positive and appreciative of the university faculty presentations and PDSN efforts. Many teacher and administrator evaluations had limited written comments, such as "Thanks!" and no comments were negative or critical of the presenters or session content. For example, Tim Merritt facilitated four sessions and received 36 anonymous teacher and administrator evaluations on "Smarter PC Use," and every written comment was positive.

Although the evaluations measured participants' reactions, it is nearly impossible to isolate the effects of a single activity (Guskey, 2002). Also, in the absence of other measures, the conference evaluations show very positive levels of initial satisfaction. Many evaluators noted how they wished the sessions were longer. One educator wrote, "I enjoyed the class so much that the session ended and I was not ready to go." And another participant unmistakably expressed a positive reaction to the session, "Great job! Very well organized and well presented. Love the new tips." An evaluation of Janet Burns and Jessie Hayden's session highlighted some of the concerns espoused by teachers as a result of misconceptions or previous university experience. "I thought it might be too research-based and not practical, but this was [the] best reading session I have ever been to." Similarly, one teacher wrote, "Dr. Ariail was really great. I liked that she opened with the theory and ended with the practical application." Clearly, university participation in professional development has built bridges with the high school and explicitly shown that university professors are productive and "practical" collaborators in promoting student learning.

Many of the professional development sessions focused on pedagogical strategies to improve student learning. A vital dimension of effective professional development (especially for math and science) is helping teachers understand the ways students learn and the content they teach (Guskey,

2003). The university spring Professional Learning Conference session titles and faculty presenters were as follows:

Using HEI to Engage Students during Test Preparation —Mr. John Pecore

Performance-based Mathematics Tasks —Mr. Neal Christian

Smarter PC Use —Mr. Tim Merritt

Practical Strategies to Improve Literacy Skills —Dr. Janet Zaleski Burns and Dr. Jessie W. Hayden

Co-teaching in the General Education Classroom: Foundations and Must-Have Conversations —Ms. Joanna E. Cannon

Going 'Round in (Literature) Circles —Dr. Mary Ariail

Presenters Benefitted too

The university presenters also benefitted in many ways when they shared their expertise and collaborated with practitioners. Some recognized the importance of improving teacher practice and student learning. One presenter wrote, "The conference helped me to recognize how interested in-service teachers are to learn new teaching strategies that have the potential to raise student test scores." Tim Merritt expressed the mutual benefit of professional development presentations in the following statement:

> For me, it's always useful to get a sense of the real classroom issues that teachers face when using technology. I find real value in helping teachers—showing them how to save time and stress with good keyboard shortcuts, or ways to use multimedia to drive home the point of a lesson. If I can help them feel confident about technology in their classroom, they'll feel like more effective teachers overall. (Personal Correspondence, 2009)

In an unexpected and thoughtful gesture, GHS offered stipends for all the university presenters. Yet all the presenters initially declined their stipends and expressed gratitude for the opportunity to share their passion and expertise with the teachers and administrators. All university faculty presenters showed commendable devotion to the PDS partnership, teacher quality, and student learning. According to Guskey (2003), "educators at all levels value opportunities to work together, reflect on their practices, exchange ideas, and share strategies" (p. 749).

In addition to the Professional Learning Conference and through a similar commitment to the PDSN partnership, Harley Granville and Dr. Susan Ogletree from the Education Research Bureau at the university committed their time and grant writing skills to facilitate three grant writing workshops. The principal requested the workshops to assist GHS with seeking external funding. One GHS department chair reported that the first two grant writing workshops were the most productive and valuable workshops that he had attended in over three years!

SUMMARY

In summary, our professional development initiatives were the result of close collaboration across university departments and school systems in an effort to meet the needs of the teachers in our professional development sites. We drew on the knowledge, values, interests and expertise of our partners and on the research in the field regarding professional models that have been shown to yield results (Loucks-Horsley, Love, Stiles, Mundry & Hewson, 2003). As illustrated by the stories in this chapter and in other chapters in this text, our collaborative efforts provided specialized opportunities to advance professional development with partner schools. As Lin Black highlighted, our CCLC initiative showed strong increases in teacher satisfaction, retention, and student achievement. In addition to advances through CCLCs, Lou Matthews and Kezia McNeal Curry utilized professional development opportunities to enhance culturally responsive pedagogy and multicultural education for high-need schools. Both approaches to professional development helped teachers to understand and engage their students in content instruction that was rooted in the students' cultural norms and lived experiences. Through Curry's utilization of action research, teachers investigated their practice and examined student work to improve instruction, collaboration, and student learning. As Joseph Feinberg described earlier, PDSN enhanced communication between school and university faculty, which enabled close collaboration to leverage resources and expertise for a number of professional development opportunities.

This chapter highlights the many and varied approaches to implement successful, relevant, and timely professional learning experiences through PDSN. By working with faculty from universities and schools to broker a range of activities to meet the needs of specific sites, we have ensured that our professional development opportunities provide diverse experiences across the network. Through close collaboration and a shared vision on the importance of increasing student achievement, we found ways to prepare and support both in-service and pre-service teachers.

REFERENCES

· 2007–2008 Report Card, (Gilbert–pseudonym) High School. *The Governors Office of Student Achievement.* Retrieved March 3, 2009, from http://reportcard2008. gaosa.org/(kfdwvn45hdzfhk21grglo2u2))k12/demographics.aspX?ID=667:1 87&TestKey=EnR&TestType=demographic

Banks, J. A., & Banks, C.A.M. (Eds..) (2004). *Handbook of research on multicultural education* (2nd ed.). San Francisco, CA; Jossey-Bass.

Drago-Severson, E.E. (1994). What does "staff development" develop? How the staff development literature conceives adult growth. Unpublished qualify paper.

Enyedy, N., Mukhopadhyay, S., & Danish, J. (2006). *At the intersection of statistics and culturally relevant pedagogy: Potential and potential challenges of learning statistics through social activism.* Paper presented at the International Conference on the Teaching of Statistics. Retrieved January 17, 2006, from http://www.gseis. ucla.edu/faculty/enyedy/PUBS/communit_mapping _v15.pdf

Guskey, T. R. (2003). What makes professional development effective? *Phi Delta Kappan, 84,* 748–750.

Guskey, T. R. (2002). Does it make a difference: Evaluating professional development? *Educational Leadership, 59*(6), 45–51.

Gutstein, E., Lipman, P., Hernandez, P., & de los Reyes, R. (1997). Culturally relevant mathematics teaching in a Mexican American context. *Journal for Research in Mathematics Education, 28*(6), 709–737.

Irvine, J. J., & Armento, B. J. (Eds.). (2001). *Culturally responsive teaching: Lesson planning for elementary and middle grades* (1st ed.). New York: McGraw-Hill.

Ladson-Billings, G. (1994). *The Dreamkeepers: Successful teachers of African American children.* San Francisco: Jossey-Bass, Inc.

Ladson-Billings, G. (1995a). But that's just good teaching! The case for culturally relevant pedagogy. *Theory Into Practice, 34*(3), 159–165.

Ladson-Billings, G. (1995b). Toward a theory of culturally relevant pedagogy. *American Educational Research Journal, 32*(3), 465–491.

Ladson-Billings, G. (1997). It doesn't add up: African American students' mathematics achievement. *Journal for Research in Mathematics Education, 28*(6), 697–708.

Leonard, J., & Guha, S. (2002). Creating cultural relevance in teaching and learning mathematics. *Teaching Children Mathematics, 9*(2), 114.

Loucks-Horsley, S., Love, N., Stiles, K. E., Mundry, S., & Hewson, P. W. (2003). *Designing professional development for teachers of science and mathematics.* Thousand Oaks, CA: Corwin Press.

Lutkus, A. D., & Weiner, A. W. (2003). The nation's report card: Trial urban district assessment, mathematics highlights 2003 [Electronic Version]. Retrieved August 23, 2007, from http://nces.ed.gov/pubsearch/pubsinfo. asp?pubid=2004458

Matthews, L. E. (2003). Babies overboard! The complexities of incorporating culturally relevant teaching into mathematics instruction. *Educational Studies in Mathematics, 53*(1), 61–82.

Morrissey, M. S. (2000). *Professional learning communities: An ongoing exploration.* Austin, TX: Southwest Educational Development Laboratory.

National Center for Education Statistics. (2006). *The nation's report card: Trial urban district assessment, mathematics 2005* (No. NCES 2006–457r): U.S. Department of Education.

National Council of Teachers of Mathematics. (2000). *Principles and standards for school mathematics.* Reston, VA: Author.

Nelson-Barber, S., & Estrin, E. T. (1995). Bringing native American perspectives to mathematics and science teaching. *Theory Into Practice, 34*(3), 174–185.

Stein, M.K., Smith, M.S., Henningsen, M.A., & Silver, E.A. (2000). *Implementing standards-based mathematics instruction: A casebook for professional development.* New York: Teachers College Press.

Sparks, D., & Loucks-Horsley, S. (1989). Five models of staff development. *Journal of Staff Development, 10*(4). Retrieved from http://www.nsdc.org/news/jsd/sparks104.cfm

Sparks, D., & Loucks-Horsley, S. (1990). Models of staff development. In W. R. Houston, M. Haberman, & J. Sikula (Eds.), *Handbook of research on teacher education.* New York: MacMillan.

Tate, W. F. (2004). Engineering a change in mathematics education. In D. Nalley, K. DeMeester & T. Hamilton (Eds.), *Access and opportunities to learn are not accidents: Engineering mathematical progress in your school.* (pp. 5–7): Unpublished monograph prepared for the Southeast Regional Consortium (SERC)@SERVE and presented at the National Alliance of Black School Educators (NABSE) and The Benjamin Banneker Association (BBA) Summit: Closing the Mathematics Achievement Gap of African-American Students, Washington, DC.

Teitel, L. (2003). *The professional development schools handbook: Starting, sustaining, and assessing partnerships that improve student learning.* Thousand Oaks, CA: Corwin Press, Inc.

CHAPTER 9

PARTNERSHIP BUILDING IN A CONTEXT OF CHANGE

Joseph Feinberg, Julie Rainer Dangel, and Chara Haeussler Bohan
Georgia State University

In the literature on professional development schools (PDSs), university faculty members often find it helpful to reflect upon their experiences working in schools (Hovda, 1999; Teitel, 2003; Tom, 2000). A professional development school (PDS) is a natural setting in which to examine and reflect on change, including the successes and struggles related to the context. PDSs also provide a context for considering how theory works within the reality of actual practice. In this chapter, you hear the voices of three professors of education working as PDS liaisons in three different urban schools (one elementary school and two high schools). We reflect upon our experiences in the context of change created by the PDS partnership and the reality of continual change in schools. Our process of reflection began with a meeting to discuss common features of our experience. We then put our individual reflections on paper, using the common features as a guide. Next, one author analyzed the written reflections, looking for commonalities in our experience. Using this process, we identified three broad categories of change: (a) at the personal level, (b) at the school level, and

Clinical Teacher Education, pages 147–159
Copyright © 2011 by Information Age Publishing
All rights of reproduction in any form reserved.

(c) in teacher preparation. These categories are used for the organization of this chapter.

We are faculty in a large, Research I, university with a strong urban mission and geographic presence. Two of us (Chara Haeussler Bohan and Joseph Feinberg) are in our third year in the role of university liaison and the other (Julie Rainer Dangel) is in her fifth year. During this time, we have varied responsibilities as we acculturate to our respective PDS environments. In many ways, partnership building in a context of change is predominant in our work.

The following sections describe our experiences, including frustrations that are at the heart of managing change in three different professional development schools (PDSs). We begin with a brief discussion of change in the PDSs, and follow with a general examination of the challenges posed by frequent change in education. Second, we explore change as it particularly relates to professional development schools. In subsequent sections, we describe our particular realities with respect to change in areas common to partnerships: relationships, roles, communication, governance, school climate, and teacher preparation.

CHANGE IN PROFESSIONAL DEVELOPMENT SCHOOLS

A growing body of research is developing with respect to change in education. When sifting through research on change, two distinct paths emerge. The first is specifically related to change theory, which Connell and Klem (2000) simply define as "a theory of how and why an initiative works" (p. 94). They further add that the change must be plausible, doable, testable and meaningful. Other researchers offer alternative conceptualizations of change theory. Contemporary research in revolutionary change theory conceptualizes change as a "punctuated equilibrium" which includes long periods of stable infrastructure where there is incremental adaptation and brief periods of revolutionary change (Gersick, 1991). These definitions have several implications for PDS work in schools, where theoretical research meets the practical reality of work in urban schools.

Our PDS initiative provides a structural framework for change, because it establishes structures to facilitate a new kind of partnership between PK–12 schools and universities. There are several reasons a framework for change can be effective. Using the Connell and Klem (2000) criteria, our PDS network was both plausible and doable. The school districts and the university partnered together to develop a plausible grant and implemented it in specific schools that met a needs criteria. The grant structure was complex and facilitated many changes, but from the prospective of the three authors, the "doable" change was that university professors spent one day a week working in PK–12 schools, rather than reporting to the university. In order to test the success of the grant, surveys were conducted at schools yearly, and test data were gathered from the districts to determine if there were gains in student achievement at PDS schools in comparison to similar non-PDS schools. The last criterion Connell and Klem (2000) state is important in change theory is that it be meaningful. Foremost are explicitly stated outcomes that can create powerful learning (Phillips, 2005). In our PDS work at the three schools, we were keenly aware of the stated goal of the partnership, which was to improve student achievement. Not all the PK–12 teachers, however, are attuned to this specified outcome. As liaisons, we found our role sometimes involved informing teachers about this important purpose of the partnership. With respect to Gersick's (1991) definition of change as punctuated equilibrium, the authors certainly experienced highs and lows in the school settings. There were times when we facilitated incremental change, and there were other times where we participated in dramatic change, such as the writing of the PDS initiative into a school charter.

A second line of research on change emphasizes the challenges that accompany change in education. Building on the work of previous scholars of educational change, Hardy (2008) notes that all change involves loss, anxiety, and struggle. He recommends that school districts develop a culture where change is embraced, which he believes is critical for schools' viability in the 21st century. High-performing districts tend to demonstrate an ability to embrace change because they more often employ shared decision-making strategies, take responsibility for the education of students, and build human resources to promote student achievement (Hardy, 2008). As will become evident in the descriptions of our PDS work, the three PDSs in which we work experience varying degrees of success with respect to embracing change.

The PDS initiative is one of many reform plans designed to enhance teacher preparation and PK–12 schools. The PDS model is uniquely situated to improve student learning and enhance the preparation and professional development of educators (Teitel, 2003). Such innovation through the PDS system has the potential for transformative change in urban schools.

According to Teitel (2003), a transformative change model requires a substantial redesign of the existing organizational structure between school and university partners for "real collaboration and simultaneous renewal to take place" (p. 64). On the organizational side, he suggests that a principal-driven structure should move toward a shared decision-making approach. In many PDS networks, shared governance is a prerequisite for school participation. One flaw of the transformative approach is that it assumes stable organizational structures but limits agency afforded to individual actors. In contrast, other authors argue that individuals may have a more positive impact on student achievement than research results and organization change theory predict. Kochan (1999b) suggests that individual commitment may have a greater impact on preparing teachers and improving schools. Individuals create and maintain organizational structures and strategies rather than relying on the structures and institutions to support their work (Kochan, 1999b). The results from Kochan's study show positive change processes through several strategies, such as "developing strong collaborative relationships, being persistent, and gaining personal commitments" (1999b, p. 186). In the following discussion, we share our perspectives as university PDS liaisons related to both individual or personal and organizational levels of change. Within these two domains, we organize our experiences into six areas of PDS work: (a) developing relationships, (b) strengthening communication, (c) identifying our roles and expertise, (d) participating in school governance, (e) sharing space, and (f) understanding school climate. While each area is presented separately, you will see considerable overlap among each of these categories. When appropriate, we share promising practices that enhance our work. We conclude with our experiences in teacher preparation, a major component of the partnership, and recommendations for others contemplating PDS work.

Based on their review of the PDS literature, Lyons, Stroble and Fischetti (1997) describe changes that a university, its schools, and faculty need to consider in an age of PDS reform, including faculty identity, roles, responsibilities and work environments. They conclude that change is not easily observable and often fragile. These descriptors clearly match our observations and perceptions.

As mentioned earlier, there were three broad categories (change at the personal level, change at the organizational level, and change in teacher preparation) in our reflections with multiple subcategories that help define our thinking. As we present these categories and subcategories in a linear manner to enhance clarity, please note the overlap among each of them. For example, attending meetings was important for developing relationships, strengthening communication, and participating in school governance.

Change at the Personal Level in Partnership Work

People are one of the most integral constituents of any partnership. When considering this component of our partnership work, we find developing new relationships requires time, shared tasks, and communication—both formal and informal. We also find identifying new roles and expertise as equally important.

Developing relationships. As liaisons for PDS sites situated in urban environments, we are faced with developing new relationships. As a new person in a school where most people know each other already, we must find ways to get to know teachers and administrators. Our relationships with teachers and administrators are built and strengthened during time spent together. Naturally, PK–12 personnel are very busy, so finding time to develop and strengthen the relationships can be difficult. In our experience, we find that participating in formal meetings (e.g., leadership teams, local school advisory boards, and strategic planning committees) is critical to developing professional relationships with PK–12 faculty. They provide a formal environment for exchanging ideas, making announcements, and asking questions. These meetings are also important in our reflections on organizational change.

Informal communication is equally important. This happens in classrooms, teacher lunchrooms, departmental offices, student cafeterias, and hallways after or between classes. Sometimes our relationships are based on a few minutes of conversation from multiple encounters in the hall, during a planning period, or at lunch. The lunchroom, depending on the teachers present, is often a place of productive conversation. We find this is one place where many connections are made with teachers. Teachers advance ideas and make personal inquiries during informal conversations that they are not as likely to share in formal meetings.

In either context, the role of working with site-based coordinators and administrators provides an opportunity to develop connections and foster collaborative relationships. Tasks such as facilitating placements for interns bring university faculty and PK–12 teachers together with a common goal. Planning presentations and attending PDS conferences provide another avenue for close interaction. In our experience in elementary and high schools, we develop rapport with teachers by volunteering to help in their classrooms; working together with children makes us feel more connected.

In our experience, the strongest relationships are with site coordinators and high school department chairs. Teachers who host our interns provide another source of relationships. Similarly, teachers involved in our graduate programs and graduates of our programs, who take positions in the PDSs, allow us to build on previous connections and develop new relationships and collaborative opportunities. Thus, some change in teacher personnel actually benefits our work, as open positions provide opportunities for our interns to become employed once they have gained certification. On the other hand, drastic change in PK–12 faculty presents challenges as new relationships need to be forged and experience needed to mentor interns becomes sparse.

Personnel turnover at our school sites and at the university means that we need to develop a wide array of working relationships, nurture existing relationships, and cultivate new ones. Each of our schools experienced new site coordinators (sometimes one each year), which moved this particular sample of PDSs further away from transformative change. As site coordinators can change rapidly, a working relationship with the administrative team is important as well.

Strengthening communication. The PDS partnership facilitates change because it creates a need for communication between distinct institutions as they work together toward common goals. As noted earlier, both formal and informal sharing and communication occur and relationships are strengthened in the process. Communication and sharing often occurs during leadership meetings and meetings with administrators and high school department chairs. At these gatherings, we hear the ideas and concerns of the teacher leaders in the school and we volunteer thoughts and opinions, when appropriate. The relationships we develop with many of the teachers provide an atmosphere where they are comfortable sharing their opinions and concerns. The majority of our time at the schools is spent visiting, meeting, or informally conversing with teachers, administrators, and interns/student teachers (which often includes observing and conferencing). As university professors, we are viewed as safe outsiders, and teachers and administrators can openly express concerns about people, policies or actions. Because we are on the school campus only once a week, email communication is also critical, as it provides a way to stay in touch and accomplish tasks remotely. Yet, changes in communication structures and routines (such as email addresses, reporting structures, etc.) also present challenges. As previously noted, challenges arise in communication when the personnel of the PDS change and new perspectives are brought to the decision making process. Some of the challenges are overcome through communication and our role as university liaisons.

Identifying roles and expertise. To develop a PDS site for clinical teacher education means adding new roles to the school structure, for example university liaisons and site-based coordinators. As we reflect on the new structure of PDS work, we find change to be the norm. Like the high-performing schools that successfully embrace change, we are learning our roles and how to anticipate and welcome change. Principals and administrative teams change, university liaisons and site-based coordinators change, school governance changes, and space for PDS work changes. In all three of our sites, there have been major changes in school administration, primarily at the principal level. School liaisons often change each year, and only one of us has been in our current position as a university liaison for more than three years. In fact, within the PDS partnerships at our university, the three of us possess longevity, as liaisons at other schools can change annually and upon occasion mid-year. Despite the high number of changes in PDS players, the relationship between our PK–12 schools and the university remains stable because of the personal and professional relationships we have built with teachers and administrators.

Our PDS partnership requires new roles in the university and PK–12 schools by creating a new position, the university liaison, which ordinarily would not exist within a school. Often, the role of university liaison is seen as a person who possesses expertise with respect to teacher development. Each of us embraces our roles as facilitators who bridge the expertise and needs of the university with the expertise and needs of the school. In our experience, we find commonalities in the expertise university faculty are asked (and are not asked) to provide. Often, teachers view university faculty as experts with respect to matters of initial teacher preparation. Therefore, the most frequent use of our expertise is through our work with student teachers and interns. We have direct and specialized knowledge of our pre-service teachers and cooperating teachers that facilitates making meaningful placements and mentoring for our pre-service teachers. We are consulted when issues of interns or student teachers arise. These issues can include concerns about future employment or challenges that they face in managing learning environments or in preparing for instruction. At the request of administrators, the PDS site coordinator, and teachers, we often organize informational meetings, workshops, and communication between student teachers/interns and their mentors or cooperating teachers.

Our knowledge of university faculty and programs provides another form of expertise. We are able to provide professional development or recommendations for professional development from our university contacts. For instance, one high school liaison coordinated faculty presentations for an in-service conference and a grant-writing workshop provided by the College of Education's Research Bureau. In another instance, an elementary school liaison arranged for professional development related to teaching science and children's writing. In addition, teachers and administrators ask us general questions about university programs, particularly if they are considering advanced degrees. A common frustration for all of us is that we are not seen as resources for teaching. On rare occasions, a few teachers have asked advice about pedagogical ideas. More frequently, teachers and administrators consider us for tasks, such as creating brochures or judging the spelling bee.

In reflecting on our roles as researchers in our professional development schools, the struggles become more obvious. One of our roles and areas of expertise as faculty is as researchers. Despite action research project proposals, funds for research, and efforts to rally teachers, we are not convinced of teachers' receptivity to conducting research, or the extent of their belief in the credibility of research findings. In many cases, enthusiasm for research is minimal.

On the more positive side, we do have access and permission to conduct research, and there are a few research projects ongoing. One of us works closely with the social studies department chair on an investigation of the use of primary source documents in an AP psychology course. Another investigates the approaches to teaching practiced in PDSs and habits of handwriting in a kindergarten classroom. Nevertheless, research is relegated to a small fraction of the work we do as university liaisons, largely because conducting research requires organizational changes, a willingness to change routine habits, a commitment of extra time, and engagement in studies with unknown outcomes. While some teachers are happy and open to try new ideas in the classroom, not all teachers are able or comfortable with using their classroom as a place to conduct inquiry. Our role as researchers is based on developing professional relationships, sharing and communicating, as mentioned earlier, as well as participating in school governance and enhancing school climate which we discuss next.

Change at the Organizational Level in Partnership Work

In addition to change at the personal level, organization level change is equally important in our partnership work. Participating in governance activities, sharing space, and understanding school climate are three specific areas common to our experiences.

Participating in school governance. School governance in each of our three schools shifted with leadership changes. We observed positive and negative changes as a result of new and transitional principals, who sometimes adopted supportive or contradictory and antagonistic positions towards the PDS model. For example, the new principal at one site valued principal-driven governance and dismantled the shared-governance practice; he also questioned the value of remaining in the PDS system. At another school, a new principal embraced the PDS model and asked the university liaison to serve as a keynote speaker at the school's professional development day. Including partnership work as part of a school charter is one example of radical transformation in school governance by one PDS site; at a minimum this ensures the partnership will continue despite the constant changes.

Meetings, despite the time they involve, are key components of governance and our PDS work. Schools have as many meetings as universities; however, the purpose and topics of discussion are quite different, and our experiences are equally different. While one of us feels invited to attend, another is expected or required to attend, and a third is excluded. Principals are most often the gatekeepers for these meeting. School dedication to the partnership is often evident in the way that our liaison role is viewed. We agree with Teitel (2003) that a shared decision-making approach is essential to foster the organizational change required for successful partnerships. In our experience, meetings where all voices are heard strengthen relationships.

Our time attending meetings does not always seem productive, yet it is the one place for us to bring up ideas, voice an opinion, build relationships, or share our expertise. It is interesting to note that just as meetings may seem non-productive to us, teachers also question their relevance. When there is so much to do in the classroom, is a meeting a productive use of time? Just as teachers report having responsibilities that take them away from their classrooms, we wonder how to balance our responsibilities in PDSs with the need to make national presentations, conduct research, and write for publication. While meetings may appear time-consuming or un-productive, or the conversations irrelevant, our participation in them is es-sential to being a part of the school culture.

As liaisons, we all try to offer helpful advice or ask relevant questions when discussions of issues arise at leadership meetings. In listening, we do learn a considerable amount about the real issues that schools find impor-tant. Several specific experiences offer promise. For example, our involve-ment in strategic planning with the schools appears to have promise for integrating the goals of both institutions. Participation in book groups with the leadership team offers another opportunity to share ideas. As men-tioned earlier, the nature of these meetings may change as administrators and leadership styles change.

Sharing space. On a smaller scale, space for PDS work is also important. Space needs within schools change annually and largely depend upon stu-dent enrollment. We find space is often at a premium; an office is a luxury and shared space or a desk in the corner is often standard. Finding space to teach university classes at a PK–12 school requires a creative use of space.

The university provides us with a computer and printer for the PDS site; it is making this space inviting that offers promise. The following anecdote from one high school shows one possibility.

> Initially, the PDS office was shared with a technology coordinator at the school, but he changed schools. In the third year of the grant, the office became exclu-sively PDS. Upon encouragement, the interns have taken control of the office and technology resources and made it their own. One intern placed a coffee maker, microwave, and small refrigerator to give the office a lounge appear-ance. We have active discussions about teaching situations and strategies, and they frequently use the office for coffee and breaks during planning.

At another high school site, the school administrative team proudly created a small office for PDS work from a very large foreign language closet that in former times held large audiotapes and big equipment for listening to recordings. Student interns from the university use this space for monthly meetings across subject area disciplines, and the interns also use the space as a quiet place to accomplish work, such as lesson preparation or grading. In each of these examples, sharing space facilitates relationships, communi-cation, school climate, and ultimately teacher preparation.

Understanding school climate. In our experience, we notice a relationship between the success of our PDS partnerships and school climate. Climate at our PDS sites ranges from "exceptional," where people seem to like each other and their work, to "stifling" due to a top-down administrative approach. In all cases the principal (or lack of) contributes to the positive or negative climate. On the positive side for one site, teachers take on extra responsibilities to make the school and children's lives better. There is continual professional development (as part of the charter and the strategic plan for the school) and teachers seem to enjoy learning. At this school, the principal honestly believes the partnership is an asset to the school, and it is included in the school charter. She is often heard championing the partnership to parents, teachers, and the community. The school is welcoming to university students (often hosting a breakfast) and other university visitors. On the negative side, one site struggles with effective leadership, a high attrition rate for teachers, and a lack of enthusiasm for the work of schools. After a failed attempt to hire a university graduate, this principal attempted to dissolve the partnership.

Another influence related to school climate is the shifting demographics in the area. It is difficult to teach when the student mobility rate nears 60%. The populations of our schools are transient and they represent multiple ethnicities and nationalities. The metropolitan area has experienced white flight and tremendous growth over the years, and the neighborhoods have changed accordingly. Our schools used to be located in what was considered suburbs, but because of the rapid growth of the city, they have become more urban and centrally situated. To facilitate their effectiveness, one school is a magnet school and another is a public-conversion charter school. Overall, the teachers who remain in our schools are positive about teaching and dedicated to their students, despite demographic changes and frustrations related to school climate (leadership, students' tardiness and absenteeism, lack of parental involvement, etc.). Sharing a mission to enhance urban education strengthens our PDS collaboration. Having a partnership between schools with urban demographics and a university focused on the needs of diverse students is a reciprocal relationship with positive influence on teacher preparation; together the work is easier.

Teacher preparation. Strengths of the PDS partnership between the university and our PDS sites are the commitment to teacher preparation and attending to the personal and organization levels described above. Research shows that PDS-based teacher preparation programs (as compared to campus-based programs) develop teachers who are better prepared for their first year of teaching (Ridley, Hurwitz, Hackett, & Miller, 2005).

There is a willingness on the part of most teachers to accept student teachers from the university. The university benefits by having a place for student teachers to learn their craft, and schools benefit by hosting young professionals who often have creative and energetic goals for teaching. Through the PDS partnership, we successfully place interns from a diverse group of subject areas, such as language arts, math, science, fine arts, counseling, health and physical education, and social studies at the middle and high school level and early childhood and special education at the elementary level. Between ten and 20 students are placed at each school each semester. The school administrators are pleased with their performance, and we frequently receive positive comments from the teachers. Ideally, university student teachers obtain jobs teaching at a PDS after completing their internships. Schools have the opportunity to observe a student teachers' work, and if there are teacher openings, university student teachers are often among the top candidates for teaching positions.

While teacher preparation is an area of positive change for both PK–12 schools and the university, it often does not feel like growth. There are still instances where teachers only request interns for the extra help they provide; and if the interns need extra help, teachers do not reciprocate. In some cases, teachers are not very interested in improving their skills as mentors and a few find the responsibility overwhelming. While many teachers routinely support the interns, after multiple years of partnering, some teachers decline to have an intern placed in their classroom. There are varying reasons teachers decline interns, but the climate of testing is a critical factor in teachers increasing reluctance to share instruction.

On a small scale, teacher education courses are being taught in our schools. The ability to have site-based courses is often based on aspects of change mentioned above, such as available space, faculty expertise, and strong communication. While our data is limited at this point, this idea offers the potential for deeper change. Sharing the role of teacher preparation is one the most visible and significant areas of change for our university and our schools.

CONCLUSIONS

In this chapter, three individuals committed to improving student learning through a PDS model describe their experiences as they work in the changing context of PDS partnerships. Change is inevitable when working with any public agency and higher education institutions, and PK–12 school districts are especially susceptible. In our experience, we identify change at the personal or individual level, at the organizational level, and in teacher preparation. Given these changes, it is important to anticipate change and to have conversations continuously around roles and responsibilities. Based on our experience, we can make several recommendations.

- Develop relationships.
- Strengthen communication.

- Identify roles and expertise.
- Participate in school governance.
- Share space.
- Understand school climate.
- Commit to teacher preparation

Kochan (1999a), a university professor and educational administrator in a PK–12 school system, compares working in a PDS partnership to "riding the roller coaster of change" (p. 319). Indeed, there are sharp ascents and rapid declines that derive from working together in a PDS site. Kochan (1999a) observes that the down periods are counterbalanced by the highs, the times at the crest of the ride when the entire amusement park is visible, when working together individuals recognize that they are in the midst of something greater than themselves. We find that the professional development school work is worth the ride.

REFERENCES

Connell, J., & Klem, A. (2000). You *can* get there from here: Using a theory of change approach to plan urban education reform. *Journal of Educational and Psychological Consultation 11*(1), 93–120.

Gersick, C. (1991). Revolutionary change theories: A multilevel exploration of punctuated equilibrium paradigm. *The Academy of Management Review, 16*(1), 10–36.

Hardy, L. (2008). Change happens. *American School Board Journal. 12–15.*

Hovda, R. (1999). Working on a public school calendar: Personal reflections on the changing role of a university faculty member in a professional development school. *Peabody Journal of Education, 74*(3/4), 85–94.

Kochan, F. K. (1999a). Professional development schools: Riding the roller coaster of change. *Peabody Journal of Education 74*(3/4), 319–321.

Kochan, F. K. (1999b). Professional development schools: A comprehensive review. In Byrd, M., & McIntyre, D.J. (Eds.). *Research on professional development schools: Teacher education yearbook VII.* Thousand Oaks, CA: Corwin Press, 173–190.

Lyons, N., Stroble, B., & Fischetti, J. (1997). The idea of the university in an age of school reform: The shaping force of professional development schools. In M. Levine & R. Trachtman (Eds.), *Making professional development schools work: Politics, practice, and policy* (pp. 88–111). NY: Teachers College Press.

Phillips, J. C. (2005). Powerful learning: Creating learning communities in urban school reform. In Ponder, G. & Strahan, D. (Eds.). *Deep change: Cases and commentary on reform in high stakes states* (pp. 87–106). Charlotte, NC: Information Age Publishing.

Ridley, D. S.; Hurwitz, S.; Hackett, M. R. D., & Miller, K. K. (2005). Comparing PDS and campus-based preservice teacher preparation: Is PDS-based preparation really better? *Journal of Teacher Education 56*(1), 46–56.

Teitel, L. (2003). *The professional development schools handbook: Starting, sustaining, and assessing partnerships that improve student learning.* Thousand Oaks, CA: Corwin Press, Inc.

Tom, A. (2000). How professional development schools can destabilize the work of university faculty. *Peabody Journal of Education, 74*(3&4), 277–284.

ABOUT THE CONTRIBUTORS

Mary Ariail is an Associate Professor at Georgia State University (GSU) in Atlanta, GA. She holds a Ph.D. in Language Education and an M.Ed. in Middle School Education, both from the University of Georgia. Her area of expertise is Language Education, with an emphasis on issues of identity, adolescent development, reading, and children's literature. Dr. Ariail is currently serving as Associate Chair of the Department of Middle/Secondary Education and Instructional Technology at GSU, overseeing all initial teacher preparation programs and supervising program evaluation for the department. In addition to her work at GSU, she has taught at the University of Texas (Austin) and Texas Women's University (Denton).

Gwen Benson has been Associate Dean of School and Community Partnerships at Georgia State Uinversity College of Education since January of 2002. Her current work focuses upon enhancing the results of urban high-need schools by constructing multiple tiers of support. Her initiatives are guided by the need for pre- and in-service teacher support, leadership support, the recruitment of new teachers from underrepresented populations and improved PK–12 student achievement. Prior to Dr. Benson's appointment at GSU, she worked with the Georgia DOE where she served as Coordinator of the Low Incidence Disabilities Unit. Further experience includes Director of Educator Preparation (GPSC), Director of the Program for Exceptional Children, and faculty at Southern University at Baton Rouge, and Louisiana State University. She holds a doctorate from the University of Kansas.

Clinical Teacher Education, pages 161–167
Copyright © 2011 by Information Age Publishing
161

Linda Black was the Project Manager for the National Commission on Teaching and America's Future/Georgia State University Induction Project. The Induction Project offered training to teachers from those schools having an established relationship with Georgia State University (PDS) in facilitating a learning community designed to support and mentor beginning teachers in high needs schools. Before joining the project, Ms. Black served as the Director for the Metro West Georgia Learning Resources System (GLRS), a special education teacher, parent and student agency in Atlanta, Georgia. During the twenty years she spent with the agency, Ms. Black provided staff development to educators throughout Georgia, wrote several support manuals for GLRS patrons, and coordinated metro consortia made up of administrators and college faculty members who dealt with areas of concern in the field. She also became certified as a Strategies Intervention Model (SIM) Trainer for the University of Kansas Institute for Research in Learning.

Chara Haeussler Bohan is an Associate Professor in the College of Education at Georgia State University. Having studied under O.L. Davis, Jr., she earned her doctoral degree at The University of Texas at Austin. She has published articles in *Theory and Research in Social Education (TRSE)* and *Social Studies and the Young Learner (SSYL)* and has authored a book titled, *Go to the Sources: Lucy Maynard Salmon and the Teaching of History* (Peter Lang, 2004) and edited a book titled *American Educational Thought: Essays from 1640–1940* (IAP, 2010). She is currently an Executive Editor of *The Social Studies,* a Taylor and Francis publication.

Donna Breault is an Associate Professor of Educational Leadership at Northern Kentucky University. Her research focuses on Dewey's theory of inquiry and its implications for curriculum, leadership preparation, and higher education administration. Donna has authored *Urban Education: A Handbook for Parents and Educators* (Greenwood Press, co-author Louise Allen) and *Experiencing Dewey: Lessons for the Classroom* (Kappa Delia Pi, co-author, Rick Breault). In addition, she has articles published in a number of journals including *Educational Theory, Educational Forum, Educational Studies, Planning and Change,* and the *International Journal of Leadership in Education* (in press). Donna is currently working on two books: *Red Light in the Ivory Tower: Contexts and Implications of Entrepreneurial Education* (Peter Lang, co-author, David Callejo-Perez) *and Researching Professional Development Schools: Lessons from the Field* (Rowman and Littlefield, co-author, Rick Breault).

William L. Curlette is a Professor in the Department of Educational Policy Studies and the Department of Counseling and Psychological Services at Georgia State University. He is a Diplomate in Adlerian Psychology and is Co-Editor of *The Journal of Individual Psychology.* He has consulted for over thirty years with school systems and foundations in the areas of program evaluation and research methodology. Within the last six years, he has been a co-principal investigator on two federal grants related to professional development schools.

Kezia McNeal Curry is an instructor at the University of Hawaii at Manoa, where she teaches in the Middle Level Masters of Education (MLMED) program and the Institute for Teacher Education (ITE). Previously, she was an Assistant Professor of Middle Childhood Education at Georgia State University. She holds a Ph.D. from Emory University in Educational Studies with an emphasis in Multicultural Education. Her research interests include culturally relevant interdisciplinary professional development, middle-level education, culturally responsive pedagogy, and health. As a military spouse, she is also especially interested in the unique educational needs of military children. Through her consulting company, Global Kaleidoscope, she is currently focusing on two projects: the examination of the generational transfer of teacher knowledge, and K–12 students' intersections of health science and culture.

Julie Rainer Dangel is a professor in Early Childhood Education at Georgia State University and currently coordinates the doctoral program in early childhood. Her research interests include teacher development and constructivist theories. She has published articles in a variety of journals including *The Journal of Teacher Education, Teaching and Teacher Education* and *Policy and Practice in Education* and is a past-president of the Association for Constructivist Teaching. She has served for seven years as the university liaison at a Professional Development School in a large urban district.

Mary P. Deming is an Associate Professor of Language and Literacy in the Middle/Secondary and Instructional Technology Department at Georgia State University. She is the co-author (with Maria Valeri-Gold) of *Making Connections through Reading and Writing* and has had her work published in the *Journal of Basic Writing*, the *Journal of Adult and Adolescent Literacy*, and the *English Journal*. Her research interests include teacher quality, alternate teacher preparation, and university-school partnerships. She was the co-PI of a 6.5 million dollar Teacher Quality Enhancement Grant titled PDS2— Professional Development Schools Deliver Success.

Caitlin McMunn Dooley, Ph.D., is an Assistant Professor in the Early Childhood Education Department at Georgia State University. She has written widely about issues related to teacher education and development as well as literacy development and early instruction. As a proponent of professional development schools and clinically based teacher education, Dooley is the principal investigator (PI) or co-PI for grants totaling more than $14 million that support professional development, school networks, and service learning in P12 schools. Professional recognition and awards from the International Reading Association, Association of Literacy Educators and Researchers, Literacy Research Association, and the Georgia Association Teacher Education attest to Dooley's contributions to the fields of literacy and teacher education. Her most recent publications can be found in *The Reading Teacher, Action in Teacher Education*, and the *Journal of Early Childhood Literacy*, among others. Dooley currently serves as co-editor for the journal *Language Arts*, sponsored by the National Council of Teachers of English.

Joseph R. Feinberg is an Assistant Professor of Social Studies Education at Georgia State University. He taught social studies at Campbell High School in Smyrna, Georgia, where he received the Martin Luther King Humanitarian Award. Joseph earned his doctorate degree, education specialist and masters degree at The University of Georgia and his bachelor degree from UNC Chapel Hill. He recently served four years as a PDS university liaison for a local high school. His research interests include teacher education, simulation games, civic education, and service learning.

Teresa R. Fisher is a Clinical Assistant Professor at Georgia State University, coordinating the Early Childhood Education/Teach For America Urban Teacher Development Collaborative. Fisher, who spans the boundary of the university/school partnership, previously worked as a first- and second-grade teacher in one of the university's professional development schools before joining the Georgia State Faculty first as a doctoral fellow and then as a Clinical Assistant Professor. She has served as the Reading and ESOL endorsement instructor for PDS in-service teachers in two counties. Additionally, she has served as the program coordinator and instructor for two graduate-level initial teacher preparation programs in Language and Literacy and in Early Childhood Education. In these contexts, Fisher's research has focused on reconceptualized collaborations for urban teacher development as a means for social justice, both locally situated and broadly constructed. Specifically, she has joined pre-service and practicing teachers, inquiring into their practices and pedagogies and worked to create and maintain partnerships with schools and nonprofits to foster teacher development for critical change.

Joyce E. Many is a Professor of Language and Literacy Education at Georgia State University, where she serves as the Executive Associate Dean of Academic Programs in the College of Education. She joined Georgia State after serving on the faculty at Texas A&M University and as a research fellow at Northern College in Aberdeen, Scotland. Her research has concentrated on understanding children's literacy processes and the classroom contexts that shape those processes, on exploring factors impacting teacher education, students' performance in literacy education courses, and, most recently, on describing the scaffolding processes teacher educators, teachers, and peers use to support student learning. Dr. Many served on the Board of Directors for the National Reading Conference from 2001–2007 and is currently serving on AACTE's Research and Dissemination Committee.

Lou Edward Matthews has been actively involved as a community organizer, scholar and speaker, where he has engaged audiences of leaders, parents, teachers and students, as well as professional groups throughout the United States and in Bermuda over the last 20 years. He is currently serving as the Director of Educational Standards and Accountability for the Department of Education in Bermuda, where his major responsibilities are ensuring and supporting all schools in attaining excellence for all children in Bermuda's public schools. Dr. Matthews has taught at middle school, high school, and college levels since receiving Bachelor of Science degrees in Mathematics and Accounting from Atlantic Union College in 1991. Subsequently, he obtained a Masters of Education in Secondary Mathematics from Alabama A&M University in 1994 and a Ph.D. in Mathematics Education from Illinois State University in 2002. He has written journal articles and book chapters on the subject of culturally relevant teaching, mathematics education, and black masculinity.

August E. Ogletree is a Research Associate for Atlanta Public Schools, where she works conducting research and evaluation for system initiatives. She received a Bachelor of Arts in Educational Studies from Emory University and a Masters of Arts in Early Childhood Education at The University of South Florida at Tampa. She completed her Ph.D. in Educational Policy Studies in 2009 at Georgia State University. She taught elementary school prior to earning her Ph.D. and continues to serve school systems in the Atlanta Metro area. Her research interests include effective teacher preparation, mathematics and science pedagogy and professional development schools.

Susan L. Ogletree is Director of the Educational Research Bureau at Georgia State University. She holds a doctorate in Educational Policy Studies with a focus on Research, Measurement and Statistics from Georgia State University. Her primary research interest is professional development schools and their impact on academic achievement. She is Co-Principal Investigator for the Network for Enhancing Teacher Quality (NET-Q) $13,500,000 grant which works with 6 urban districts and 2 rural districts around implementation of Professional Development School Programs.

Laura Smith has been an Assistant Professor in the Department of Early Childhood at Georgia State University since 1994. She completed her Ph.D. in Elementary Education at the University of South Carolina. Laura's primary focus is educating future teachers to teach in grades Pre-K through

5th. Her areas of expertise include mathematics education and utilizing technology for teaching and learning with young children. She has 24 years of teaching experience in early care, middle school, high school, and the college level. She also serves as the assistant coordinator of field experiences and school partnerships for the Early Childhood Department.

Susan Swars is an Associate Professor in the Department of Early Childhood Education at Georgia State University. Her teaching includes elementary mathematics methods and content courses for undergraduate and graduate students. She also serves as a University Liaison to a local Professional Development School (PDS). Her research interests includes teacher development, particularly in the contexts of mathematics education and PDSs. This research has examined how elementary teacher preparation experiences, features, and contexts impact teacher change, specifically as related to prospective teachers' content knowledge and beliefs. Recent journal publications (2009) are in the *Journal of Teacher Education, Journal of Mathematics Teacher Education, International Journal of Teacher Development, Action in Teacher Education, International Journal of Social Research Methodology: Theory and Practice,* and *Journal of Mixed Methods Research.* Recent editorial work (2009) includes serving as lead editor on the *Proceedings of the 31st Annual Meeting of the North American Chapter of the International Group for the Psychology of Mathematics Education.*

Dr. Dee Taylor, a retired PK–12 Curriculum and Professional Development Executive Director, is a major advocate of school-university partnerships. She continues to serve this passion in her current position at Georgia State University. She currently serves as the project director at Georgia State University for two major College of Education grants: (1) The *Professional Development Schools* (known as PDS)—a $6.1 million dollar grant—designed to recruit, develop and retain high quality teachers in high need urban school districts, and (2) NETQ *(Network for Enhancing Teacher Quality)*, the largest grant awarded the College of Education ($13. 5 million dollars; the 5th largest TQP award among the twenty-eight in the country). The grant serves 29 urban and rural Georgia school districts. Her experience includes English teacher, reading specialist, district-wide leadership as curriculum coordinator for middle/secondary reading, English/language arts curriculum coordinator, assessment and accountability coordinator, academic achievement coordinator, and national professional developer. She was invited to serve as on the Expert Advisory Panel for the new Georgia Performance Standards in English/Language Arts. She has been instrumental in several district-based university leadership cohorts. She continues to work with alternative teacher certification initiatives, teacher intern/resident and mentor training, and Georgia's Professional Standards Commission Review Panel/Board of Examiners. She has served in numerous state and national leadership roles for major educational organizations (NCTE/writing advisory chair, GCTE/president, GA–ASCD/diversity chair, GA Language Arts Supervisors/president). She is also an author and developer of instructional materials.

Dr. Brian Williams is an Assistant Professor of Early Childhood Education at Georgia State University. His work is situated at the intersection of science education, urban education, and education for social justice. More specifically, he is interested in the ways in which equity issues related to race, ethnicity, culture, and class influence science teaching and learning and access to science literacy. In addition to his research, Dr. Williams has over 15 years of experience working with teachers and students in science education. He has taught and presented his work to the educational communities around the world. His work has been published in *Democracy and Education, Negro Ed Review,* and *International Journal of Social Research Methodology.* Dr. Williams holds degrees from Emory University (Ph.D., 2003), Georgia Institute of Technology (M.S., 1996), and Norfolk State University (B.S., 1994). He is also a former Ford Foundation Fellow and Spencer Fellow.

CPSIA information can be obtained at www.ICGtesting.com
Printed in the USA
238251LV00002B/3/P

9 781617 354236